A HISTORY OF MISBEHAVIOR

PIRATES, PICKPOCKETS, PROSTITUTES, AND
PARISHIONERS IN COLONIAL SAVANNAH

GRACE FLEMING

Three Sheets
PUBLISHING

For permissions, please contact the publisher at threesheetspublishing@gmail.com.

Artistic contributions by Lucy Robbins-Rice and Matthew Austin

CONTENTS

ACKNOWLEDGMENTS

I have had the good fortune to know many talented people who are always willing to lend a hand. Without them, this book would not have been possible.

A big thank you to Bethany Robbins, Mary Fleming, Laura Kasserman, and Glenna Cunningham, who put up with my several requests for proofreading and advice.

I owe a debt of gratitude to many Armstrong State University professors who sparked my love for research and writing. Specifically, I would like to thank Richard Nordquist for his generous guidance and input.

I'd also like to remember Mark Finlay for his friendship, wisdom, and humor. He is greatly missed.

Finally, I thank my husband, John Glimmerveen, for his constant support and for years of enduring the many messy stacks of research. He probably thinks they're going away now.

INTRODUCTION

On an early morning of July, 1732, a dozen of London's elite gentlemen readied themselves for an important meeting at the Georgia office in the Old Palace Yard. Adorned in hand-knitted stockings, silk garters, and high heeled shoes, the Georgia Trustees would debate a proposal by James Edward Oglethorpe concerning the unsettled southern region of the Province of Carolina.

Mr. Oglethorpe hoped to establish a new settlement in this wild region, which would serve a few good intentions. The new colony of Georgia would provide a fresh start for some of London's imprisoned debtors, but it would also serve as a buffer zone for Charleston, a valuable asset to the crown that lay vulnerable to attacks from Spanish Florida. After much debate, the trustees agreed to finance the venture, with a few alterations to Oglethorpe's original plan. Instead of settling the land with debtors from London's cruel prisons, they decided to populate the colony with a group of deserving poor from the boisterous, crime-filled streets of London.

This book aims to provide insight into the origins of

modern Savannah, the charming, haunted, oddball gem of the American South. The decision to settle the hostile land with ill-prepared city dwellers would ensure that the colonists provided proper roots for the city of Savannah: they were an eccentric mix of elegant rogues and lovable weirdos who attacked the swampy environs armed with street smarts, blunderbusses, and rum punch. Grandparents to the ball-gown crowd of the 1790s, these original settlers cleared the trees and built the first wooden dwellings on the bank of the Savannah River, and squabbled, cursed, and drank their way into a unique chapter of colonial American history.

1

HEAD SMACKS AND HORSE PARADES

It was a cold November day when Savannah's future citizens gathered at Gravesend in England, an ancient town on the River Thames. They clutched their bundles, their lock boxes, and their loved ones, and carefully boarded the small ketches that would carry them to the *Ship Anne*. Many of those first colonists would have known in their hearts that they were seeing England's waters for the very last time. But the passengers had every reason to take this risk, leaving their homeland to set off for a strange place in the wilderness somewhere south of Charleston. For among these travelers were the very poorest of London's population, and for the very poor, existence in London was brutal and cruel. East London in the 1730s was characterized by filthy, open sewers, starving, abandoned children, free-flowing gin, and dangerous criminal enterprises.

The poor side of London town was such a dangerous and dastardly place, that *proper* citizens were advised to avoid it at all costs. Pickpockets and prostitutes, beggars and bag snatchers, vagrants and villains—they lurked in every shadow.

While the crowd that strolled to the river to set off across the Atlantic were happy to leave London behind, it would turn out that some of those infamous street scoundrels were the very ones to populate the new settlement called Savannah. In fact, within the first five years of Savannah's settlement, among the first people to inhabit Savannah, four colonists were indicted for running a brothel and one was convicted of lewd living. Three of the settlers were fined for scandal, four were indicted for theft, a few were murdered, and a few more were hanged for committing murder. But before all those shenanigans could take place, and many more instances of misbehavior could occur, that original group had to survive the long and brutal journey across the Atlantic.[1]

Walking the Plank and Other Fun

The Atlantic voyage, itself, showed signs of dysfunction to come. Before the ship left Gravesend, the river pilot, whose job it was to guide the ship to the open sea, was fired for drunkenness. The crew who were hired to sail the ship were a rude and rowdy bunch, not much removed from pirates. For some reason, they disliked and abused the Savannah bound passengers—seemingly for their own amusement. In fact, one of the sailors decided to show his lack of respect for Oglethorpe by throwing his companion dog overboard.

Their cruelty was widespread, and the crew ridiculed, tormented, and abused the passengers at every opportunity— even throwing a bucket of water on mourners who gathered when a voyager died at sea. At one point, a few of the passengers neglected to pay the ship's captain a bottle fee, and they were forced to walk the plank—sort of. The accused were tied up by rope, lifted up by the yard arm, and dangled over the water while the rest of the passengers watched in a mix of horror and amusement. They were spared a dunking, but only after they promised to clean the sleeping cradles. This threat of a dunking was apparently a common one, since another man barely escaped walking the plank for giving a sheep's head to the dogs on board, but he was pardoned in the nick of time by Mr. Oglethorpe.[2]

Interestingly, the crew members weren't the only ones to have fun at the passengers' expense. When passenger Anna Coles was reported to have slapped her husband around for some unknown offense, the entire ship came together to celebrate in beer-fueled merrymaking. Public humiliation was a form of great entertainment in the early 1700s, and, as luck would have it, there was an entire ceremony dedicated *specifically* to tormenting a henpecked husband. The ship's passengers did not let the opportunity escape. They performed a traditional ceremony, called Riding the Skimmingtons, and this specific spectacle involved many intricate details.[3]

First, the passengers set up a parade, in which they would mock the distressed couple in effigy. One man dressed up as the husband and another man dressed as the wife. The two men perched on a horse (the horse could be real or manufactured from available materials) with the "husband" turned backward to face the horse's backside. The "wife" wielded a large spoon that she used to strike the fake husband while onlookers cheered. The crowd carried signs and played drums and any other available instruments. This all came together to form a dysfunctional, celebratory procession around the town—or, in this case, around the ship. It is not known whether Mr. and Mrs. Coles attended the ceremony, or if they stayed below deck while the rest of the passengers had their fun.

If the two did skip the grand celebration, they also missed out on the game-playing that commenced afterward. Passengers followed up with a game called cudgel. In this game, two men would arm themselves with sticks or clubs. The object of the game was to see which man could cause the other man's head to bleed first. The role of the onlookers was to watch for the first sign of head blood. The first to correctly call out "Blood!" was deemed the winner of the game. The winner was awarded a prize—in this case, it was a pair of shoes offered by Oglethorpe.[4]

Torture and torment were all the rage in the 1730s. In a game called Riding the Skimmingtons, a crowd humiliated a henpecked husband and his nagging wife.

Living on Board

The passengers had to find some way of entertaining themselves, because daily life was not all that exciting. Food was boring and rules were strict, since some modicum of law and order was needed to keep everyone safe. Families were divided into small groups, and a leader was chosen for each. One role for a group leader was to make sure all candles were put out by eight o'clock at night. After that time, passengers would settle in to their cradles below deck in complete darkness, hearing the creaks of the wooden hull and the sound of the crashing waves. They'd surely bolt upright with the feel of an occasional big wave and ponder the many fathoms of dark sea beneath them. At one point, passengers were kept below deck in the heat for three days, and several became violently ill (perhaps from the smell). Oglethorpe sent them a few bottles of wine to appease them.

The small groups they created were also handy for making sure meals were doled out in an equitable way. Each group would receive a bundle of beef and plums on Mondays, Wednesdays, and Fridays. On Tuesdays and Thursdays, it was pork and peas, while Saturday was fish day. A few weeks into the trip, carrots were given out. In true Savannah fashion, every person over twelve received two quarts of beer a day. Beer was a good replacement for the rum-laced water, which turned dark and tasted foul after a few weeks, but sadly, the beer also turned bad and tasted sour after a few weeks. All in all, most of the passengers survived the journey. But there were times when they must have questioned their sanity for making this move.[5]

Chased by a Pirate?

Once the *Ship Anne* had completed its voyage across the Atlantic, it was necessary for the vessel to wait offshore near South Carolina for a local sea pilot to come out to board the boat and perform navigation through the local waterways until it reached shore. The *Ship Anne* was boarded, but was most likely delayed a bit longer while they waited for favorable tide and wind. It was at this point that the passengers—

before even stepping foot on Savannah soil—may have encountered their first pirates.

As the *Ship Anne* huddled outside the coast, the man on watch detected another boat on the horizon. It was a sloop, he noticed, the very type of boat that pirates preferred. It appeared to the watchman that the sloop lurked in the distance for a time before changing course and heading directly for the *Ship Anne* and its boatload of future Savannahians. The man called an alarm, and the deck was soon flooded with concerned passengers.

Upon observation, Mr. Oglethorpe declared that the approaching vessel must be a pirate ship, intending to plunder them. He ordered all of the men to fetch their arms, although it was later noted that a few of the men who'd previously proven to be bullies "skulked" below deck as the events unfolded.

Oglethorpe asked the women to make sure that all spare weapons be carried up, and requested that they and their children return below. Many of the women insisted on staying on top and helping as they were able, though.

The sloop continued to bear down on the *Anne*, and the ship's captain ordered everyone to hold fire until he gave word. Once the sloop was close enough, the captain ordered a shot to be fired across the stern, but the shot appeared to fall ahead of the sloop. They fired another shot on the apparent pirate ship, and this one landed much closer, which caused the charging sloop to lower its sail. Now the two ships drifted close to one another, and the would-be attackers could see that the deck of the *Anne* was filled with armed men. After a time, the mysterious vessel lifted sail, turned about, and departed.

Long after the event had passed, one of the city officials debated whether the aggressors had truly been pirates, or if, instead, the culprits were Spanish scouts from nearby Florida. The local pilot who had boarded the ship claimed that it was, in fact, a known pirate in the local waters. Whatever the true identity of the attackers, it would not be the last encounter of either, for Savannah continued to face incursions from both Spanish spies and piratical sorts, for many years to come.[6]

Dry Land

After a time, the travelers were carried from their initial landing spot in South Carolina to a site that Oglethorpe had scouted for the new colony. The settlers were carried up the alligator-infested Savannah River to the high bluff where River Street now thrives with tourists. The first nights were fraught with challenges. Colonists, once they landed on the shores of the Savannah, were warned early on that "they must lye without Cover" in tents "till they could build Houses for themselves." They were advised to eat "salt Meat, drink Water, work hard, and keep guard for fear of enemies." They were informed that the country was going to be unimaginably hot in summer, and there were flies and ferocious insects in abundance. Not surprisingly, the trustees' warnings would hold true: the days and months to come would reveal that there were insects and perils aplenty.[7]

It couldn't have been very restful to sleep in the stuffy tents, crawling with bugs and smelling from the unwashed, for weeks on end—especially in the knowledge that the surrounding woods had eyes. Countless, mysterious dangers lurked just out of sight, so it must have been a very long week until the time that every family was finally armed with a musket and bayonet, cartridge box, and belt.

There were more ships to come, of course, with more eager and optimistic souls who believed that a new life in Savannah would be preferable to a life of poverty in the crime-ridden environs of London. The London-based Georgia Trustees continued to interview applicants who were interested in finding a new home abroad.

One unsuccessful pair of applicants sheds some light on the process of interviewing and choosing new Savannah prospects.

A man approached the committee along with his wife, begging to be sent to Savannah and provided passage and a plot of land. As repayment, the man promised to improve his land with cultivation and carry out volunteer work to build up the town. When the committee turned him down, the two offered to go, instead, as indentured servants, in effect, to "sell" themselves to someone already established in Savannah. Upon investigation, the committee found the two unfit to labor as servants. The reasons had to do with the wife. As it turned out, she was the "bastard daughter to the Earl of Carlisle," who had swindled her father a few times. She'd been promised ten pounds a year to disappear to Jamaica, but she took the first ten pounds and didn't follow through with her promise. The Trustees suspected the woman was merely attempting to swindle them, as well, and it was observed that she was, at that very moment, wearing a silk gown that was "very pretty and airy." It was determined that the couple was not deserving of charity nor compassion. It is a pity that she did not make the cut, since it turned out, with her charms, her conniving ways, and her penchant for misbehaving, she would have represented Savannah perfectly well. But there were plenty of others to carry the torch.[8]

The Original Rogue

On one of those vessels that followed the *Anne*, was a dastardly cad named William Wise. This was a con man of alleged nobility—at least he claimed to be a noble. What is certainly clear, is that this particular man was a rogue who had applied for his passage to Savannah because he had squandered all of his inheritance. Interestingly, this man's personal story foreshadows Savannah's own ultimate character, because this man, in addition to being an eccentric oddball, was also the colony's first murder victim.

Mr. Wise boarded the ship with a woman whom he claimed to be his daughter. As days progressed, his amorous and scandalous behavior toward this woman generated a lot of concern and a great deal of outrage. After all, living quarters were quite impersonal, with only a hanging canvas to separate passengers as they slept on their swinging cradles. Gossip spread like wildfire when the two displayed some rather indecent affections. After some time, a few sharp minds deduced that the woman was not *actually* the man's daughter.

Meanwhile, back in London, officials soon caught on to the scheme, when they realized that one of London's most talented prostitutes had disappeared. They put the puzzle together to conclude that the woman had boarded the ship with Mr. Wise under false pretenses. There was an attempt to catch up with the ship to remove the pair, as the vessel made its way from one supply dock to another, but the ship was well out of reach quickly, and the attempt failed. Meanwhile, stories of the shock and horror caused by Wise and his alleged daughter lingered at every port.

Mr. Wise made it to Savannah and built the first settlement on Hutchinson Island. It is not clear whether the woman stayed in Savannah, but she likely moved to Charleston, where there was an established prostitution industry.[9]

2

THE PEACEKEEPERS

Thee was no standard police force in colonial towns, at least not a force as we know them today, and much of the peacekeeping was up to volunteers from the general population. In early Savannah, the law and order system was often lawless and usually disorderly. The town was originally divided into sections, smaller than the town squares, called tythings. Each section had a head tythingman whose job it was to organize volunteers from his block to keep the peace. The volunteers were called night watchmen. These watchmen would stay up all night, walk the streets, lantern and rattle in hand, and make sure all was well.

All home-owning men were required to serve on the night watch, but these first peacekeepers were hard to manage, as it turned out. The men complained constantly about the requirement to serve, since they were exhausted from the hard work of clearing land and building their houses during the day. As a result, they often failed to show up for their assigned posts, and this left the streets unmanned and unprotected. When that happened, the tythingmen would retaliate in any means they could. A certain Mr. Mouse wrote to General Oglethorpe to complain that his tythingman had tied him by the neck and heels as punishment for missing one night of duty.[1]

Sometimes, tythingmen, themselves, ended up on the wrong side of the law. In 1738, one Patrick Grant, "who was a weak Man, but conceited in his own Opinion," displayed a "pert and saucy Behavior," when he affronted the judges (called bailiffs or magistrates) and refused to obey their orders. In return, the bailiffs saw that he was "very deservedly committed to Gaol [jail]." But rest assured, poor Mr. Grant was not alone in his insubordination. At some point, men from nearly every station and level of the law in Savannah spent a night or two in jail.[2]

A night watchman would patrol the streets with lantern in hand.

Gradually, more peacekeeping officials were added to help with the duties of law enforcement. The position of constable was added along the way, and this official was responsible for delivering warrants and carrying people off to jail.

When it came to the court system, there was plenty of drama in early Savannah. A panel of three bailiffs was assigned to oversee court cases, with the position of first bailiff being the most powerful. This highest official had the ability to sway the other bailiffs, as well as the grand jury members, who were selected from the small Savannah population. For their service, the second and third bailiffs were paid twenty pounds a year, while the first was paid thirty pounds.

At first, it was difficult for the bailiffs to command the respect that was needed for them to carry out their jobs, since they were merely plucked from the general population and had no real experience for the job. For that reason, the Trustees sent them ornate, purple robes to wear in the courtroom.

The courtroom was a large building in Wright Square that doubled as the church. The three bailiffs (also called magistrates) sat in the front of the room in their large, white wigs and brightly colored, fur-lined robes to make judgements on accused criminals. The poor defendants relied solely on testimonies for their own defense, as there were no lawyers allowed in Georgia at this time. The first courts also had a recorder, who managed the time with hour glasses and kept the court's records with quill pen in hand. John Pye served as an early recorder, although he was accused of being a spy for the people at one point.

Savannah's very first bailiffs must have enjoyed the robes and the authority that came from running a courtroom, but there were signs that the authority went to their heads. Despite their power and fancy dress, they did not necessarily impress the citizens of the town. At one meeting of the court, officials discussed the scurrilous papers that had been "fixed up in Public places, by persons unknown, scandalously reviling the Magistrates and others, as abusive and malicious Libels." The court expressed their discontent at the shocking accusations and went about their business, though likely in a disgruntled state.[3]

Complaints surfaced that courts were called too often in the early days, with defendants being raked into court for a variety of offenses, which put even more of a time constraint on them, as well as the poor citizens who were forced to serve as jurists. Juries were a rare feature for Colonial America, for in many colonies, juries were not used; it was too difficult to assemble jurors from the far corners of the county. Nonetheless, Savannah did require citizens to serve on a jury and it did cause some push back, since it was taxing on those who toiled endlessly, battling weeds and trying to grow crops in marshes every available minute. To make matters worse, after all their time and effort, the verdict of the jury was not always respected. At one point, Thomas Causton, the chief bailiff, reportedly dismissed the entire jury for making a judgement that annoyed him, claiming they were a bunch of fools and blockheads who had no understanding of the law.[4]

Causton was a wildly unpopular man. He was often accused of cruel and sneaky behavior, and he was known to spy on citizens and skulk around beneath windows to eavesdrop on potential wrongdoers. As chief law enforcer, he was known for whipping and torturing people at will. Torture became the norm under his reign, although it was also appreciated as a source of entertainment for bored townsfolk.

Causton was not simply the most powerful bailiff; he was also the town storekeeper, a role that allowed him to make decisions about who could acquire food and tools from the Trustee's store. In his role of storekeeper, citizens accused

Causton of playing favorites with provisions, letting some people go hungry because they displeased him. In the meantime, Causton, himself, was making enough money that he could somehow afford the finer things in life. While many people struggled, one man complained that Causton always "shows up now in ruffles and his house is well furnished."

Not surprisingly, through the first several years of Savannah's existence, the trustees received many complaints about the unprofessional behavior of Causton and the other bailiffs. Mr. John Dobell complained in a letter to the trustees that the magistrates spent a great deal of their time "Carousing in Taverns, and Jaunting about from place to place, a Singing and Dancing, insomuch that Savannah has been left without any Magistrate from Monday to Saturday." One by one, like most people in early Savannah, the very officials who oversaw the court proceedings found themselves on the opposite side of the bench, defending themselves against a range of offenses, from bad behavior to criminal charges.[5]

Trading Places

One of the complaints in Savannah, whenever someone was arrested, was the people tasked with keeping law and order were no better than the criminals. It is true, that the bailiffs, constables, and other men of political power did occasionally break into fisticuffs with their neighbors, and they did fail to enforce laws against the public selling of rum at their favorite public houses. These pubs, places of merriment among the English, must have been a high building priority in the new settlement, since a few were established within a few short years of Savannah's existence. While they were often places of scandal and mischief, Savannah pubs also became hangouts for officials, who joined in for some merrymaking from time to time. One Monday evening, Bailiff

Parker decided to visit one of his regular establishments for a bit of refreshment. It was a drinking house in Ellis Square, owned by his friend Mr. Jenkins.[6]

The rum flowed freely, it seemed, when Parker and Jenkins decided to amuse themselves by putting on a show for the other patrons of the pub. In exchange for a free rum punch (the most common drink in Savannah), Parker agreed to exchange identities with Jenkins, the publican. The two men stood before the cheering crowd and stripped away their clothes. They exchanged their garbs to dress again and pretended to be one another. Jenkins, pretending to be a bailiff, ordered a drink, but Parker, pretending to be the owner of the shop, refused to serve him because he was too drunk. In return, the fake bailiff offered some verbal abuse, "calling him a drunken Swab and other opprobrious names," to the joy of the onlookers. He then upped his game by throwing Parker to the ground.

The act may have entertained most of the crowd that night, but it also prompted a letter of complaint to the Trustees by one indignant observer.[7]

Killing a Priest

To a great extent in the 1730s, many English colonies were not very tolerant of Catholics, in general, and anti-Catholicism was particularly heavy in Savannah in those earliest days, where the greatest threat to the colony came from Florida Spaniards who prowled the woods and the coastline. Perhaps that is why, when Mr. John Brown faced trial for killing a priest in 1737, a fracas erupted.

While the details of the priest's death are not known, it is possible that the death may have been the unintended consequence of an ill-timed, surprise meeting with a Spanish priest in the woods or at sea. After all, the town was in a quasi-war

with Florida from the earliest days. What is very clear was
the fact that half the town, including several lawmen, were
determined to derail the legal proceedings and put an abrupt
end to Mr. Brown's troubles.

Patrick Grant was serving on the grand jury that investigated the alleged killing, so he was one of the men deciding
whether the case was to go to trial. He was strolling inno-
cently through the streets one day when he came upon Bailiff
Henry Parker, who appeared to be displeased. Sure enough,
Mr. Parker accosted Grant and directed him to put an immediate end to the legal proceedings concerning the priest, or
else Mr. Grant would pay serious consequences. Mr. Grant
refused, explaining that he had no authority to end the grand
jury enquiry. With that, Grant turned away and continued
toward the courthouse, but when he arrived, he found that
the proceedings had just been adjourned, by another jury
member, a Tythingman Hows.

With that announcement, the confused and displeased
Mr. Grant turned around to find Bailiff Parker had caught up
with him again, this time with a cane raised above his head.
Mr. Parker and a small mob commenced to beat Mr. Grant,
while a few other men pelted the poor man with scurrilous
language. Poor Grant insisted, later on, that he never raised a
fist in self-defense. Nonetheless, he was thrown into jail that
evening. But this was only the beginning of Grant's troubles.

The jail must have been in a terrible state, as Grant said
there was an "open vault of nastiness" in his cell. He was
eventually moved to another jail, where "all the lights [win-
dows] were nailed up by the express order of Mr. Causton,"
and he was confined there for fourteen days "without the
benefit of the light of the sun, moon, or starrs." He soon fell
sick in prison, but was allowed no visit by a physician. He
was held there until he signed a confession for being in
contempt of court.

Grant would later complain to the Georgia Trustees of his treatment, claiming that Mr. Parker had been "intoxicated with Liquor" upon his attack, and that the man was said to have spent that day getting drunk with Mr. Dixon, a "man of most notorious character and a notorious drunkard," although Dixon was also the town clergyman.

There is no further information and no indication that the trial for the killing of the priest ever took place.[8]

Face Down Dead

Sometimes, law and disorder in Savannah turned tragic.

Some of the people arriving on those first ships came as indentured servants. Life as a servant in Savannah could be quite brutal and unjust. Sometimes, it was deadly and, true to Savannah's nature, the consequences were downright macabre. First Bailiff Thomas Causton was strolling along Bull Street one day, chatting with a friend, when he spotted one of his servants walking along the same street carrying a gun. It was not illegal for the man to possess a gun, for many of the servants lived on the edges of town and hunted the woods for sustenance. Still, Mr. Causton was incensed at the audacity of the man, so he called out his name. The servant ignored the call, or failed to hear it; either way, the situation made Causton's blood boil. After all, how dare the lowly servant ignore the town's chief bailiff?

A chase ensued, as Causton and his sidekick pursued the man. When the servant realized that the two men were coming after him, he attempted to flee. The poor man was overtaken, and fists began to fly. The servant was beaten and carried to the logg-house jail, where he seems to have received a few more blows. He was locked away for the night.

The next morning, when the jailor opened the logg-house window, the prisoner was lying face down in a pool of vomit, apparently dead. Officials were called in—but they were the very same officials who had placed the man in the jail in the first place. A quick inquest into the death determined that the man had accidentally suffocated on his own vomit, and the case of the dead indentured servant was closed.[9]

DISORDER IN THE COURTS

Another major figure in early Savannah was Colonel William Stephens, a man whose title changed during his time in Savannah from Secretary to the Trustees to President of the Colony. For entertainment, Mr. Stephens confessed that he enjoyed sitting in on the courtroom proceedings, which could provide some amusing or downright shocking surprises. For example, in 1739, Magistrates met to find two bills of indictment for felony against two persons in prison at the time. One of the men was held for offering his wife for sale, and the other was locked up beside him for offering to buy her. The men claimed that there was insufficient evidence against them, since they refused to testify against one another. Upon examination, the magistrates ruled the case *Ignoramus,* a grand jury statement meaning that an official ruling is impossible due to lack of information.

On another pleasant afternoon of court-watching in Wright Square, Stephens casually reported that the day had seen five criminals convicted and sentenced to a stint at the whipping post. Two men were to be whipped for stealing cattle, one indentured servant was convicted for keeping secret knowledge of a robbery, one for "stealing Fowls," and one for stealing pipe staves in the woods (the parts for constructing wooden barrels).[1]

All in the Family

There were petty crimes and scandals galore to be heard in the early Savannah courts. One scheme played out like a modern day crime drama, when a poor, sickly man was brought before the jury, having been accused of theft. The victim of this crime was an upstanding woman who had come to Savannah penniless, but had managed to save up seventeen guineas in the few short years of residence in the colony. She worked as overseer of a poor house. Ordinarily, the woman kept her money safely on her body, sewn up in her garments "as the Usage of the common People."

The accused was named Mr. Brodie, and he had come to Savannah as a Scottish servant, but he had fallen ill and had been living in this indigent home under the care of the victim. During the trial, it became increasingly obvious that the poor man was in no physical condition to carry out a robbery or any form of sinister plot. What was noticed, instead, was that the woman had two daughters who "had each of them an Eye, for a while Past, on what their Mother had got."

It was soon discovered under testimony that one daughter had been recently married. This daughter took the stand to say that she had often seen old Mr. Brodie leaving the house in the middle of the night, and he did so on the very same night that the woman's money and garment had disappeared. In his defense, poor Brodie admitted that he'd been up in the night, but only to visit the necessary house, as he was suffering "under a Flux," which required many such nightly visits to the outhouse.

The daughter insisted that she could show exactly where the man had hidden the garment. She and her new husband commenced to lead the jury to a place in the victim's own yard, where they began to dig. Sure enough, the garment and its hidden contents were unearthed, exactly on the spot she suspected. The jury saw through the woman's charade, and concluded that it was she, the daughter of the victim, along with her new husband, who had actually stolen the money. As a result, Mr. Brodie, the poor, "half-witted Fellow" was acquitted.[2]

Witness Tampering

Savannah's indentured servants, whether English, Dutch, German, or other, always seemed to get the short end of things. An irascible, drunken man named Mr. Brown from Highgate was known to be "seldom sober, or in use of his reason." One day, he took his frustration out on his own servant. In a drunken fit, "with little or no Provocation, had taken his Gun loaden with drop Shot, and a Ball, and shot his Servant through the Thigh." Sadly, a gunshot wound was not the sort of injury that colonials tended to recover from, wherever the shot landed. A surgeon was called in, and it was confirmed that the news was bad. The shot did not seem survivable. Since the nameless victim was certain to die, Mr. Brown was taken into custody, and, once the servant died, indicted.

When trial day came around, Mr. Brown claimed that he had a witness who could testify that the whole incident was just an unlucky accident, and that the shot was not an act of violence after all. Unfortunately, Brown claimed, he had not been able to convince the witness to join him at court, so he would need more time to prepare his case. In a rare display of tolerance, the magistrates agreed to give the man more time to collect his witness. But days turned into weeks, and each time the court met, Mr. Brown failed to produce his witness. Finally, the court got fed up with the man's delays, and ordered him to report to court, with or without his witness.

In another turn of events, it seemed that the one witness for the prosecution failed to turn up on the appointed day. There was much rumor and speculation that the man who was supposed to testify *against* Mr. Brown had been "stifled and spirited away." Frustrated magistrates could not allow the case to go forward without their own King's witness, so they delayed the proceedings once again, this time announcing a reward of ten pounds sterling for anyone who could find their witness.

This announcement infuriated Mr. Brown. He was incensed that the court would imply that some kind of shenanigans had taken place, and offended by the announcement of a reward for the delivery of their own witness against him. He became highly "outrageous" and "publickly caused a Paper to be fixed up at the Door of the Court-House," where he announced the "illegal and arbitrary Treatment" he was suffering.

Once again, the court was not entertained by his ranting. They responded by tossing him in jail, where he could "think a little farther of it under proper Confinement." Weeks passed, but the witness would not be found. The court could only proceed on the word of the surgeon, who could not say for certain that the death of the victim was intentional. As a result, the surgeon recommended that the court find Mr. Brown guilty of manslaughter. The case was settled with a guilty verdict, but the case of the missing witness was never resolved. There were rumors that the man had been spirited away to a hideout somewhere in South Carolina.[3]

The Hog's Face Case

One of the common offenses tried on Savannah's early courts was the theft and butchering of livestock. This crime may have been particularly tempting for indentured servants, who often lived in huts in the woods outside of the main town. Livestock that was owned by town folk was frequently allowed to roam free in the woods, since there was no place to pen them up inside the town limits.

One Friday in 1738, several men were accused of stealing and butchering some cattle and a dozen hogs that belonged to Mr. Henry Parker, one of the town bailiffs at the time. Two of the accused men were landowners, and one was an indentured servant, and they were all accused of shooting the animals, cutting them up, burying their hides, and dividing the meat. During the trial, one of the land owners, a Mr. Hetherington, showed contempt for the accusation. He protested "in a very insolent and audacious manner," when asked to approach the magistrates to testify. In other words, he turned his back on the purple-robed authorities and would not face them when he spoke.

The magistrates were not amused, so they had the court officers forcefully turn him about "by a kind of violence" and obliged him to stand "by a decent posture." All of the men objected to the accusations, but the court carried on. Testimony was given to claim that a herd of hogs had wandered into Thunderbolt settlement, where the act was committed. The men, it was said, "struck" a dozen of the pigs with their guns and chased the others into the woods. They then scalded and dressed them, buried the skin, and cut them into pieces that they divided among them.

Witnesses came forward to testify that Mr. Parker's pigs were known to wander in the very woods near Thunderbolt, but that evidence was not sufficient to find the men guilty.

Mr. Parker may have lost this fight, but he managed to produce proof enough in the end. He presented to the court the face of a pig that had been buried, with its ears still attached. On the pig's ear was a mark that was identified as Mr. Parker's own brand. The accused men gave no sufficient denial when faced with this evidence, and they were found guilty. The sentencing was put off for one week.

When the court gathered again, and a sentence was contemplated by the magistrates, Mr. Hetherington, again, expressed his discontent with the proceedings. He appeared before the court "much disordered with drink" and made such a scene that he was forcibly removed from the court. He was placed into the stocks for an hour before being sent to the jail. In fact, all three of the men were sent to the logg-house jail.

But they would not be confined. Within a week, the three men broke out of jail and "occasioned much Hurlybury." Messengers were sent to the surrounding villages and people were sent out "several Ways in Quest of them." Despite their efforts, the men, it seems, were never apprehended. Years later, there was news that Mr. Hetherington had absconded back to London with his new wife—a widow Lacy, who was one of the witnesses in the trial. [4]

4

TORTURE DEVICES

Torture was in wide use as a spectator sport throughout Europe in the late 1600s and early 1700s, and definitely a part of London life. It is only natural, then, that Savannah would embrace the custom of tormenting people in the name of keeping law and order, but also in the interest of quality entertainment. While it might surprise us today to know that torture devices adorned the courthouse lawn of early Savannah, it wasn't really that surprising to the everyday colonist. In American colonies, cruelty was simply a normal part of life. But it seemed to be embraced with enthusiasm in Savannah, for the settlement earned itself a wicked reputation that was known to observers from afar. One terrified settler (who eventually fled to Charleston) described a logg-house that had become "famous in Carolina, and every where else in America." The jail, he explained, had "became a Terror to People's Minds." It was fitted out with devices to include a whipping post, gibbets, and stocks.[1]

The whipping post was not a colonial invention, of course. In fact, we have Henry VIII to thank for some of the devices used in Savannah. In his reign, a Whipping Act passed, intended to punish vagrants. Those whippings were carried out at the end of an ox cart, because the punishment would be a moving spectacle, as the criminals were often carried around on the end of the cart and "whipped about town." As it turned out, Savannah employed both the ox cart and the whipping post quite frequently through the colonial days—and beyond.

The pillory was the stand-up version of the stocks, and this device was a particularly popular one when it came to public punishment. Horse thieves could expect to "be set in the Pillory a space not exceeding Four Hours nor less than Two Hours in some Public place." For a second offense, the thief could expect a stint at the whipping post and be branded on the shoulder with the letter R.[2]

Savannah's pillory was used for all sorts of offenses. The fear of disease entering the town by way of passenger ships was a concern that grew as years progressed. By the 1760s, the pilots (whose job it was to escort arriving ships through the coastal waterways) had a separate duty: they were to board ships and interrogate the ships' captains about illness on board. If the commander or doctor on board refused to answer or lied about sickness on board, they would pay a stiff fine and "stand in the Pillory from the Hours of ten to twelve of the Clock in the Forenoon."[3]

The Unfortunate Milk Maid

A less common form of colonial punishment—one that was used in the older, New England colonies to torment women who had misbehaved in some way—was the ducking stool. Also called the cucking stool or dunking stool, this gadget was a common punishment for women whose offenses were gossiping, nagging a husband, or causing a public disturbance of some kind. For some unknown reason, in the town's very early days, the Savannah magistrates decided to sentence the town's young dairy maid to a ducking in the Savannah River. The sentence was an odd one, because the town didn't actually *own* a ducking stool. Nonetheless, this maid was to be dunked into the murky water of the Savannah, while onlookers gaped, gasped, and cheered.

Customarily, the device to be used for a ducking would resemble a playground teeter-totter (or seesaw), only instead of having a seat at each end, this device would sport a handle at one end and a chair at the other. The contraption would be positioned near the edge of a lake or river, and the guilty woman would be secured into the chair. A few strong men would grab the handle of the opposite end and raise it up to dunk the woman underwater repeatedly.

Since Savannah officials didn't own anything like this device, they had to improvise, and fashion their own version with the tools they had at hand. A ship was anchored in the Savannah River, close to the shore, so that the many interested spectators in town would have a clear viewing area from Bay Street. The young dairy maid was tied into a wooden chair, and a long rope was attached to the chair. The woman was dropped over the side, and as she dangled, the men holding the rope pumped their arms up and down, attempting to plunge the lass into the river. Sadly, the laws of physics did not operate as anticipated. Instead of dunking the poor woman underwater repeatedly, they managed only to slam her against the side of the ship with their wild gesticulations, and perhaps tipping her sideways and upside down a time or two for good measure. After a good while, it was evident that the ducking attempt was not working out as planned, and the punishment was stopped. But for the maid, it was too late, as the poor young woman was well battered and bruised. Savannah's only dairy maid was out of commission for a few months, and, surprisingly enough, later reports indicated that the town's children suffered from a lack of milk. There is no record of the offense that was committed by the young woman, but it must have been a small one. When Oglethorpe spoke of the event afterward (he was out of town when it happened), he descried her offense as a trifling one that he would have dismissed.

Surprisingly, the ducking stool, or at least the punishment of ducking, survived well beyond the eighteenth century in some parts of Georgia. In 1811, a Miss Palmer from Milledgeville, Georgia "was tried, convicted, and punished for scolding." The young woman was reported to be "glib on the tongue," and was publicly dunked into the Oconee River while onlookers gawked and cheered.[4]

Some of the unfortunate, tortured individuals came from

the higher ranks of society. In the earliest days of Savannah's settlement the residents of neighboring Carolina were delighted and intrigued by their new neighbors. No doubt, most Carolinians felt they had a great deal at stake in the success of the new colony, for it was, after all, a buffer settlement. Many successful gentlemen became benefactors of the newcomers and contributed livestock, servants, and money as a way to support the new settlement. Mr. Charles Odingsell, a man of good breeding, was one such advocate from Charleston. He'd provided the colony with a gift of cattle. At some point early on, Mr. Odingsell made a trip to Savannah to see how the colony was getting along. It was a trip he would soon regret.

The Wandering Benefactor

In their zeal to promote law and order in the young colony, the magistrates established a curfew in order to address the problem of vagabonds and wanderers who lurked about the streets at night. Unlucky Mr. Odingsell arrived in Savannah late in the evening. This was a man of consequence from South Carolina who was not likely accustomed to upstart behavior from the rabble. The poor man was heading for his lodgings when he "was taken up in the Street for a Stroller." Despite his protestations, he was sent to the logg-house jail. The man was imprisoned and tormented while the officials investigated his presence in the town. Sadly, Mr. Odingsell protested for some time before authorities saw fit to release him. But it was too late, as the trauma of being locked in a logg-house, and perhaps displayed barefoot in the dreaded stocks had proven too much for him. He was in a terrible state upon his long-awaited release, and was "carried aboard his boat in order to be sent home, and died in the Way somewhere about Dawfuskee Sound."

Often, the whipping post could be used as a symbolic setting for humiliating criminals. Sometimes prisoners were merely displayed there for hours on end, so strollers and passersby could stop to taunt or torment them further, tossing rotting vegetation and dead animals their way. This was the case of Mrs. Cundal, a woman who was forced to expose herself to shame for hours after she was caught stealing chickens from Edward Jenkins. The woman was ordered to stand two hours at the whipping post bearing a sign which told of her chicken stealing misdeeds.[5]

The Logg-house Jail

One of the earliest priorities was to build a jail in Savannah, and the first jail was commonly called the logg-house. The Savannah logg-house was probably no more than a rectangular room with rough-hewn walls, equipped with a chamber pot and a chimney. A typical log-constructed jail from colonial times had a single heavy door, a single window (or none at all), and a few narrow slats cut high on the walls, created for slipping food and necessities in and out. This first Savannah prison would be well-used and quickly dilapidated. In fact, the original logg-house was just the first of many structures designed to confine evildoers in Savannah. One settler noted that in Savannah, "Logg-Houses and prisons of various sorts were built and erased successively, and most part of them were fitter for Dungeons in the Spanish Inquisition than English jails."

While jails were difficult to maintain, jailers were difficult to keep. John Wright was both a jailer and a tythingman in 1744, when he got himself in a little scrape with the law. At some time around three a.m., for some unknown reason (maybe rum inspired), Wright and two of his comrades rushed up to the standing sentry at the Guardhouse on the edge of town. The men were wearing disguises to conceal their identities. They approached the sentry and told him they were messengers from Charleston, and they carried an express, urgent message for the officials of the colony.

Sadly, this was not an appropriate time to play a joke. At this very time, the town was under a state of alarm, having heard rumors of a pending attack from Spanish Florida. The sentry did recognize one of the men and turned them all away, but that didn't stop the rumors from flying. The story snowballed until half the town believed that there had been an actual express from Charleston, and that a Spanish attack was imminent.

At this time in Savannah's history, the colony was overseen by a President and Assistants. They were not amused by the behavior of Wright and his co-tricksters, so they sent out warrants for the men. Wright refused to be reprimanded, and behaved with insolence. In the end, he had lost his position as a tythingman, as well as a jailor. He was replaced by a man named Thomas Young.

Thomas Young was also not a very good jailor. It turned out that the prisoners under his care kept breaking out of jail, whether this was by design (with Young's help) or if it was by incompetence. Either way, Young lasted for a year or so before he was charged with "Crimes and Misdemeanors," and acts "too notorious to be passed by," and swiftly relieved of his duties.[6]

The Savannah Debtors' Prison

The thought of a poorhouse lock-up might be shocking for those mildly interested and relatively informed about Savannah's history. After all, the whole purpose of settling the colony was to give relief to the poor in London's work-houses, the history books say. But, alas, the solution for punishing those in debt was just too lodged in the culture of early eighteenth-century society, and records show that Savannah had, in addition to the logg-house jail, a workhouse where mild criminals and poor debtors could work off their obligations to society. In fact, one of Oglethorpe's first mandates was to build a large wooden building to serve as both courthouse and temporary church, "with a workhouse over against it."[7]

The separation between a workhouse and a jailhouse was a blurry one. In the late seventeenth and early eighteenth centuries, there was little difference in the minds of society between a poor person and a petty criminal, since poor people frequently committed petty crimes in order to survive. A workhouse was seen as a humane way for poor people to earn their way out of poverty, since they could serve a good purpose working for the town while paying off a debt. Even still, there were frequent complaints that Bailiff Thomas Causton was a cruel man who jailed far too many for debt. In 1735, Robert Parker wrote that he was arrested for "two trifling debts" and ordered to appear in court, and in 1738, Oglethorpe, himself, complained that ten people were currently locked up for debt and that the "Court of Savannah has taken upon them to imprison for debt."[8]

As the decades progressed and the governance of Georgia evolved, laws were established concerning the workhouse and debtors. While some were able to "find sufficient employment within the limits of the jail," others were not. Those unfortunates could take an oath of poverty to declare that they had no possessions other than their clothes, their bedding, and the tools of their trade. They could be freed to earn their way out of debt, unless their creditors objected and offered to pay them a weekly allowance of seven shillings to pay off the debt.[9]

5

PICKPOCKETS AND PROSTITUTES

s Savannah grew, more and more of London's streets were relieved of petty criminals in search of a new home and a clean record. Records show that Savannah life was not necessarily easier than life in London, when it came to basic survival, and some settlers continued their streetwise ways in the new land.

Most Respectable Suspects

In 1739, William Stephens returned from a visit to his plantation to hear some shocking news:

> At my return, my Ears were presently filled with the talk, which almost every Body had at their Tongue End, of Mr. Scrogg's being defrauded of a great Sum of Money, which it was supposed was done by picking his Pockets.[1]

The amount of money stolen was 70 pounds sterling, which, in a modern equivalent, would amount to about

16,500 dollars. The cash was carried about in a letter case, which he kept on his person. Mr. Scrogg was carrying this unusually large amount, because he was sent to carry out a mission of buying horses for General Oglethorpe. Unfortunately, Scrogg decided to visit a few of his friends before setting off on his mission.

The investigation posed a curious problem, in that all of the men who were on Scrogg's list of visitations were respectable men about town. The first place he went, he reported to be "in an Honest man's house in town," where he put up the packet, but was seen taking it up again before he went on his way.

He reported that he did not sit down anywhere or visit any pub, but he did visit three more men. "But as they were all honest men in Town, and lay under no suspicious Character, there could be no Accusation against them." Mr. Noble Jones was put on the case to play detective, since "he had good experience in detecting Roguery," but the case proved to be past his skills in determining. Thus, Savannah officials surmised that the man must have suffered at the hands of a talented villain he'd casually encountered during his strolls from place to place, and this incredible case of lucrative pocket picking was never solved.

It seems the art of picking pockets sustained a few criminals throughout the colonial period in Savannah. For example, in 1768, a pickpocket worked the crowd at a public hanging and made off with at least six pounds.[2]

Picking Pocketing Widow

It was just a few months after the first ship landed in Savannah that a woman was wandering along the riverside when she came upon a drunken man, stumbling his merry way along the street. The woman discreetly rifled through his pockets, where she found precisely what she'd hoped for, for she pulled back her hand and found eight shillings sterling weighing heavy in her palm. She absconded with the money, but her crime was soon discovered, and the woman was taken in for picking pockets.

Fearing for her life, the woman make the usual claim among women who found themselves in trouble: she claimed to be with child. While authorities could not be sure this was true, they did discover that the woman was recently arrived on the ship *Georgia Pink*, and that her husband had, tragically, been washed overboard during a storm. Savannah officials felt merciful, so they let the woman out on bail, but they threw the pickpocketed *victim* into the stocks for having been drunk on the street.[3]

The Bidding War

It should be no surprise to anybody that colonial women who found themselves alone and unprotected in Savannah took to a life of crime, and it should be less shocking that some took to the oldest profession in the world. Women did not enjoy a lot of political or social power in the early eighteenth century, but they did have the power of their charms, and it's an absolute certainty that some women used sex to survive, while others, undoubtedly, had sex because they liked sex. The shocking Mrs. Willoughby may have represented the latter.

It was 1735 when the recently widowed Mrs. Willoughby met William Watkins, and the two seemed to have an immediate, mutual attraction. In fact, they were so enamored with one another that they decided to marry pretty quickly. For some reason, Watkins found someone other than the clergyman in town to marry them, and it was never quite clear who actually could have carried out the ceremony. It may have been a very timely ceremony, because the bride turned out to be pregnant.

Sadly, that was shortly before Watkins received a letter from his *real* wife, who was "alive and well in England." This was a serious problem for the blushing bride, as she was carrying the child of a married man, and "the world would soon discover it, and believe she played the Whore." Neither of them wanted that for the Widow Williams-Wakins. As it turned out, the couple had never actually *told* anyone about their betrothal, and this might have provided them with a way out of their predicament. They devised a scheme.

Watkins played matchmaker, and convinced Richard Mellinchamp to marry the woman. She must have been a charmer, because Mellinchamp agreed right away. Now the widow was legally and properly married by the town minister —but then her new husband realized she was pregnant and announced his "misfortunes in marrying her."

It seems like the woman turned back to Watkins, as Mellichamp discovered the two of them hanging out at Richard Turner's Savannah pub. A humiliated Mellinchamp demanded that his pregnant wife return home with him, but she refused. He then announced to the pub that "he would sell such a wife for a Goat at any time." Someone in the crowd "jocularly said he would give a Shilling for her," and this declaration prompted a bidding war for the woman. Gradually, "by way of Auction she was declared to be sold for five pounds Sterling."

Mellinchamp did not seem particularly upset at having auctioned off his new wife and the wife was not particularly upset, either. He was happy to walk about with five pounds sterling. As for the pregnant bride:

 Satisfied … the woman declared she would go with the buyer and behaved immodestly. One

> Langford then in company at their desire
> conveyed them to his Lodging, where they were
> bedded in publick and the five pound paid and
> Accepted of.[4]

It was only a matter of time before the authorities heard about the story. Watkins and Langford (the man who provided the room for the liaison) were both charged with misdemeanors, and the woman was charged with bigamy. Watkins was whipped "at the Carts Tail around Town" and sent to jail. The woman was also sent to jail, the authorities showing no mercy for her fragile state. As for Mellinchamp, the poor duped groom who auctioned off his bride, he was acquitted of any wrongdoing.

Prostitutes on Parade

Bull Street was the center of life in Savannah, and most gatherings and celebrations began or ended on this noble street. The street was even the site of a few parades of an unusual nature.

When a young servant woman was taken in during Savannah's first days and accused of "seducing" other women, she was most likely, in reality, one of Savannah's first entrepreneurs, trying simply to lure other women into the lucrative occupation of prostitution. She was sentenced to a whipping at the butt of an oxen cart, but sentencing a delicate young woman to a public whipping was one thing, and carrying out the punishment was quite another. Once the ox cart pulled up to the intended location, it seems that Oglethorpe decided to intervene on this young woman's behalf. Instead of lashing the girl as an audience watched, the town settled for a lesser sentence. They skipped the whipping and settled for humiliation, by way of merely parading the woman as she sat in the back of the cart. Of course, according to custom, the event gave onlookers the opportunity to throw rotten fruit and vegetation at the criminal. Oglethorpe then had the girl immediately placed in a pettiagua (large canoe) and carried to Charleston, determined to have her "return to London to her friends."[5]

There appears to have been two women sentenced to parading up and down the street on full display. In 1735, a Miss Elizabeth Malpus traveled to Savannah under the false claim that she was married. She was not married, and when authorities made a visit to inquire about this claim, the woman was found "lying between two fellows naked." She was indicted for this crime and for leading a dissolute life and paraded up and down Bull Street.[6]

6

COLONIAL CRIMES

It wasn't long before there was a need for more serious methods of keeping order, as crimes were committed more frequently over the months, and the tythingmen and magistrates weren't trained in English law. Thomas Causton realized that he needed guidance when it came to appropriate punishment for specific offenses, so he sought advice. In writing to the trustees back in England, he inquired: "I must Desire your Directions what will be your proper judgement to give in petty Larceny, Whoredom, Adultery, or other offenses which are generally punisht by the Laws of England" with whipping, imprisonment, fines or "burning in the hand."[1]

The Hue and Cry

Since there was no established police force, the task of catching absconding criminals in broad daylight was left up to the individual citizens. Like other colonies, Savannah followed English common law as its basis for statutes. One practice that carried over to the colonies was the "hue and cry" method for apprehending evildoers. English law states that a witness to a crime must raise alarm, and "that hue and cry be duly raised and pursued against murderers, thieves, and either felons, etc." In other words, any man who witnessed a crime being committed was to call attention to the act with a shout such as "Stop! Thief!" and then pursue the culprit and attempt to make an arrest. All who joined in the pursuit of a felon were deemed under the protection of the law.[2]

The term "hue and cry" can also refer to a type of early all-points bulletin, which stands until a known evildoer is caught. When prisoners Bishop Hetherington and Thomas Wright broke out of jail in 1738, a hue and cry was enacted. In response to the proclamation, a notice was posted in the town center and word was sent to Charleston, so that people far and wide could be on the lookout. Similarly, when Charleston officials caught word of a horse thief absconding to the south, the hue and cry was posted in Savannah and spread by messenger to Fort Argyle and other military style posts to the south.[3]

Official communications in early Savannah and other colonies often came in the form of papers called broadsides. These were announcements printed on one side and read aloud by a town official—sometimes accompanied by beat of drum—before being attached to the courthouse door or onto a message post in the yard of the courthouse. The city post contained announcements about laws and criminal matters, as well as marriages, deaths, gossip, accusations, and official meetings.

Colonial Counterfeiting

In 1735, Savannah magistrates received repeated claims from South Carolina authorities that their monies were being counterfeited by someone in Savannah. At the time, each colony issued its own paper money, and each colony had its own coin ratings. Although it irked Savannah leaders, it was generally acknowledged that South Carolina paper money was worth more than Georgia money. There was a bit of tension between the colonies at this time, and the fact that South Carolina accused a Savannah citizen of making illegal copies of their paper money was a thorny issue. It was even more irksome, then, to discover that the accusations were true.

Reports from Charleston claimed that a Savannah family by the name of Mellichamp, including a widely-respected father, mother, and two sons, had been indicted for creating a rolling press and manufacturing printed bills. William Mellichamp, the father, had arrived in Savannah as one of the first settlers, under the title of gentleman. Authorities in Savannah investigated, but found the evidence to be thin, so they allowed the men to remain free on bail. Shortly afterward, the Mellichamps appear to have fled the colony.

It was not long after, that authorities in South Carolina made a discovery in the barn of a Mr. Underwood. There they found William Mellichamp and accomplices in possession of several counterfeit bills, "along with all their Utensils and engraving Tools." Mellichamp and company were being held in irons in Charleston "in order to by Tryed," along with a gang of "very vile Characters," including Mr. Turner, who was a carpenter in town. After the trial, Thomas Mellichamp, one of the sons, was sentenced to jail. The mother and other family members were expelled from the colony.[4]

Clipping

On February 23, 1738, an Irish shoemaker in Savannah was prosecuted for "clipping Spanish bits." Clipping was the crime of filing or cutting off small bits of coins that were made of gold or silver. Since coins became worn and misshapen over time, it was sometimes possible to file or clip off small pieces, leaving a coin that did not look too unusual. The clippings were compiled and melted down to be sold to a dealer in metals.

The shoemaker was caught red-handed with clippings in his pocket, so he had no defense for his actions. He was sentenced "to be three times whipped" for his crime. Next to him on the whipping post was a woman convicted for stealing a shirt, although she was only to be whipped one time.[5]

Daring Robbery

In the early eighteenth century, many of the financial accounts of businesses were managed at counting houses. These were different from banks, in that they operated more like an accounting office for a specific business. In 1765, Savannah's first newspaper, the *Georgia Gazette*, reported that their counting house had been robbed.

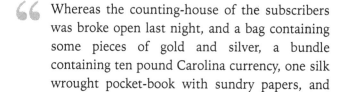

> Whereas the counting-house of the subscribers was broke open last night, and a bag containing some pieces of gold and silver, a bundle containing ten pound Carolina currency, one silk wrought pocket-book with sundry papers, and two pair of white silk hose, [were] taken out of a writing desk.[6]

An award for twenty-five pounds sterling was offered for any information leading to the arrest of the offenders.

The Gang of Villains

In 1760s, Savannah officials were aware that a "gang of villains" was traveling in the back wood regions of the southern coast, attacking and abusing settlers, stealing horses, and robbing homes. This was no small band of criminals; reports suggested that there were more than two hundred in the gang, and they had managed to "form a chain of communication with each other, and have places of general meeting." They were secretive and loyal, and they terrorized the inland settlers for years.

At one point, Savannah officials discovered that a small group of them was gathered north of the Savannah River, and they set off to capture them. Officials were somewhat successful in their campaign. In one engagement, two of them, named James Ferguson and Jesse Habersham, were killed. Two more of the gang, named Lundy Hust and Obadiah Greenage, were later captured. Those two were hanged in Savannah in the late summer of 1767.[7]

Jail Break

One of the big problems with the crime rate in Savannah was that the criminals, once captured, found it relatively easy to escape from jail. Whether it was the dilapidated state of the log house jail or the incompetence of the jailors was not clear, but it was very likely a combination of the two. Throughout the early period, news of jail breaks frequently had the community bell ringing and the marketplace buzzing with alarm and feverish chatter.

On one occasion in early Savannah, the news of a Spanish spy being apprehended and jailed had the entire town on edge. This capture occurred at a time when Savannah seemed to be on the brink of all-out war with Spanish Florida, so when authorities captured a wandering Spaniard and his Irish servant, the pair was immediately thrown in jail and put under close watch.

It seemed that nobody knew what to do with the pair, since there were no clear charges to be pressed upon the two, so the men sat in jail nearly a year before authorities began to suspect that they were plotting a jail break. Sure enough, the men attempted a break, so authorities ordered that the pair be put under close confinement and had them secured with heavy chains. After a few days, however, the chains "were found so near sawn off, that they might readily get quit of them."

This time, the outraged magistrate ordered "fresh chains," and had the men secured with belly bands. Additionally, the men were chained to the floor.

The morning after these extra precautions were put into place, the cell was found to be empty. The men had somehow escaped.

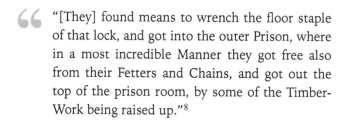

"[They] found means to wrench the floor staple of that lock, and got into the outer Prison, where in a most incredible Manner they got free also from their Fetters and Chains, and got out the top of the prison room, by some of the Timber-Work being raised up."[8]

The confounded authorities suspected the men had an accomplice, but the immediate task at hand was to catch the escapees. "Men were sent out every way on Horseback, on Foot, and by Water, to see if a discovery could be made."

Sadly, the men were later apprehended, but not before the villains were able to commit a most ghastly crime in a nearby fort. It was a murder by beheading.

7

MURDER AND EVIDENCE

S avannah is sometimes called the ghost capital of the country. How could it be so, without a good share of violent, passionate death in its history? To be sure, Savannah has had its share of macabre murders and violent incidents, and the "common hangman" was always at the ready to fulfill his duties when called upon.

Beheading at Fort Argyle

It was late at night in the shallow swamp, miles from Savannah, that Lachlan McIntosh splashed through the cypress shadows, making his way toward his small outpost on the Ogeechee River. As he approached the door of his small fortification, he was startled to see that the gate was standing ajar, unmanned. These were alarming signs, but they were not the only clues that something was amiss at Fort Argyle, for the place was eerily quiet, and there was no sign of a lamplight glowing from within.

McIntosh proceeded with caution, for Fort Argyle was one of a handful of forts built on lands surrounding the Savannah settlement, designed to protect the colonists from the many dangers that surrounded them. Since leaving London, the settlers had been warned of things that lurked in the wilderness between Charleston and Spanish Florida. Native Americans, runaways from South Carolina, wild animals, pirates, and Spanish spies, all made a home in the woods. It now appeared that the two Irish servants left alone in the fort may have fallen victim to one of these perils.

McIntosh approached the door to find his deepest fears confirmed, as the entire room was spattered and pooled with blood. All of his possessions had been strewn about the room, and his guard dog had been killed and left wrapped in a blanket. Frantically, McIntosh searched for Mr. and Mrs. Smyth, the husband and wife indentured servants who cleaned and maintained the fort. Finding no sign of them inside the structure, McIntosh cautiously searched the surrounding woods and riverbanks. After a time, he spotted a decapitated body floating in the Ogeechee water. He managed to retrieve the body, which revealed itself to be Mr. Smyth. There was still no sign of Smyth's wife. McIntosh, knowing well that the culprits could be close by, mounted his horse again and began the long, twenty-mile journey to Savannah.

It was morning when a frantic, bleary-eyed McIntosh reached the home of Peter Gordon, a Savannah magistrate. He must have sounded a bit crazed as he recounted the events of his night to the startled Gordon, because he was closely monitored while a team of townsmen traveled to the fort to investigate. They also searched the area surrounding Argyle, but they could not find the body of the missing woman. The men gathered evidence and the headless body and returned to Savannah.

There was one clue that provided some insight to the possible culprits. As the murderers ransacked the place, they stole a writing kit, comprised of a quill pen and a box of parchment paper. Officials used this information to narrow their suspects. The culprits must have been literate to burden themselves with these items as they fled through the swamps.

Meanwhile, word spread quickly in the fledgling colony and Savannah was in an uproar. There were whispered debates about the possible identify of the murderers, with most people suspecting Native Americans. Although the townsfolk enjoyed a peaceful relationship with the local Yamacraw tribe, they knew full well that other tribes scouted in the local woods from time to time. Early records suggest that a fear of an attack lingered constantly over the town. But there was another possibility. A few weeks earlier, two men accused of being Spanish spies had escaped from the Savannah jail. It wasn't long before the town officials decided that these men were the most likely suspects. After all, they deduced, if a member of local native tribes had waged the attack, they would have taken the scalp of the man instead of the entire head. That detective work, in addition to the fact that the murderers had taken food and a writing kit from the home, convinced officials that the fugitives were the culprits, so they sent their best trackers into the woods in an attempt to find them. Sure enough, a few days later, the two escapees were found huddled in a shack, somewhere inside the South Carolina border. One was a Spaniard named Mazzique, while the other was an Irishman named William Shannon. The two confessed to killing both John Smyth and his wife.

It was soon time for sentencing the confessed killers. Both men were sentenced to death, but just before the execution was to take place, each man had the ability to say a few words and ask for forgiveness. The Irishman "died a Roman Catholick," according to his final words, but the "Spaniard professed himself a Protestant." This announcement shocked a few, since he changed his mind about his religion a few times. With the murder at Argyle, he was apparently "seeking to do some good Offices for the Spaniards, as a Spy."

While the men were sentenced to death by hanging, this punishment didn't seem severe enough to quell the frazzled nerves of Savannah's populace. Oglethorpe ordered the body of one of the dead men carried to the mouth of the Ogeechee River, where it would be strung up in a cage for all strangers to see, and for scavengers to nibble until it became a caged skeleton. The presence of the murderer's bones, suspended from a tree over Ossabaw Sound, would serve as a warning to all who passed North and South. It was this passage at the mouth of the Ogeechee, they discovered, that was used by the two murders when they made their ill-fated arrival to the Savannah area.[1]

Hutchinson Island Murder

One of Savannah's most famous early murders was the demise of Mr. William Wise, the very same cad who boarded a ship with his prostitute companion. Mr. Wise set up his estate across the Savannah River, having a house with a large field for cattle to roam. It is not clear whether he settled so far from the others because he fancied himself a nobleman, and he wanted his house to look down on the little colony, or if the fellow was so vile that he was encouraged to distance himself by separation of an alligator infested river. At any rate, Mr. Wise was discovered in his bed, dead as a doornail, where he seemed to have drowned.

It's not clear how long Mr. Wise's body remained perched in his bed after he died, but it could have been some time before the body was discovered, since the man had been sickly and bedridden for some time, and he would not have been missed in town. Because he was weak, he made use of two of the Irish transport servants recently arrived. The unfortunate Wise enjoyed his daily bath, and he liked to have the male servant, Richard White, wash and comb out his hair. For some reason White and his alleged accomplice, Alice Riley, decided to kill him one morning during a shampoo.

As White sat next to Mr. Wise and combed through his master's hair, Alice Riley brought in a tub of water. As Mr. Wise leaned over the bed side for a rinse, White took hold of the kerchief that was tied around the old man's neck and twisted "till he was almost Suffocated." Alice Riley then "took hold of ye Pole of his head & plunged his Face into the Pail of Water & being very weak it Soon Dispatched him." Riley and White apparently fled the scene, although they apparently took with them some of the dead man's belongings. The murder took place on March 1, 1734, just a few short months after a convict ship carried the Irish servants into Tybee Island.

It was some time later when two brothers were busily working a field on the outskirts of Savannah, that they spotted a man running very fast through the woods. One of them noticed that the man resembled Richard White, the suspected murderer, so they decided to give chase. The only weapons available to them were two hooks and an ax, the tools they were using to clear the field. They chased the man until he collapsed to the ground, and as they stood over him, he begged for his life. They seized him and warned him that he'd only die in the woods if they left him there, and he responded that he would joyfully die in the woods "rather than dye on the Gallows."

Sadly for him, he was sent immediately to the gallows.

The man died at the end of the noose in the regular hanging
place on the edge of town, although he declared his innocence until the end. The woman was also caught, but she
claimed that she could not be hanged because she was with
child. Her claim was true, so her execution was delayed until
she gave birth. [2]

A Hanging on River Street

It was an otherwise normal summer morning in Savannah, 1739, as the dock workers loaded and unloaded their
carts and the fish mongers shouted their inventories of last
night's catch, that an eerie sight appeared in the waters along
River Street. Between the gently rocking ships that lolled in
the tidal waves, a body appeared, and floated quietly to rest
on the shore.

Officials were gathered, and the body inspected, but the
corpse was a stranger to the locals. At first, it was assumed
that the dead man was some unlucky crew member from one
of the merchant boats resting in the river—no doubt, an
unfortunate result of the previous night's drunken escapades.
After closer inspection, however, the city recorder, acting as
coroner, declared that the death was the result of a murder.
There were two round holes in the man's chest, and they
appeared to be deep enough to have caused the man's death.

The first task at hand was to identify the stranger: in
order to do this, the town magistrates would need to board
every ship in the river and interview every crew member.
While it was a cumbersome task, the official got a break
when Captain Brixy's crew was brought to shore for questioning, and one of the crewmen took flight and disappeared
into the woods.

The next order of the investigation was to scour the ship
for clues. Two items were found on Brixy's ship that appeared

to have all the qualities of a murder weapon: one was a sharp-edged compass, and the other was a large flesh fork, a long-handled utensil used for lifting meat from a boiling pot. Upon investigation, the length of the fork tongs seemed to match the depth of the dead man's chest wounds. It was determined to be the most likely tool for the deed.

Three men were taken into custody and sent to the logg-house, including Brixy, the captain of the ship. Although they all claimed that the dead man must have drowned while attempting to swim to shore for a bit of tomfoolery, the second mate disputed the story of the men in custody. There had been a fight, the witness claimed, and all three of the men in custody (and the one who fled into the woods) had quarreled with the dead man the night before. A grand jury was empaneled, and the decision was handed to the magis-trates: the three men in custody were charged with murder.

In an attempt to get to the truth of the matter, the magis-trates interviewed the men separately, promising each man immunity for testifying against his shipmates. The tactic failed, as the men were steadfast in their claims of innocence. One of the men, Mr. Levett, seemed to be the least likely of the three to have committed the crime, since he was sickly and weak, and, according to his own testimony, had laid on the deck and slept through the events of the night in ques-tion. Like the other two, and despite his pitiful condition and the harsh conditions of the jail, he refused to implicate his crew mates.

At trial, Captain Brixy was surly and defiant. He refused to answer questions and behaved with a cocky demeanor that the jury found insulting. The Captain seemingly believed that the lack of evidence would doom the case, but he was mistaken in his estimation of Savannah and its thirst for swift judgement and harsh punishment. He and the other men were convicted and sentenced to be hanged pirate style, at a place on the river that overlooked the site where the murder had occurred.

While the jury showed no mercy for the sickly Mr. Levett, the magistrates seemed to be a little more forgiving. The jury did not believe the man's story that he had slept through whatever fracas had occurred the fateful night, but the magistrates were inclined to believe that his health was so bad that he might be telling the truth. They secretly agreed to give the man a reprieve, but not until he suffered with the certainty of his execution until the last moment.

The gallows were erected on River Street, and a crowd of seventy or so assembled to watch the event on the day of execution. In fact, the crowd size pleased the magistrates, as it was a good turnout for a town whose population was dwindling from death and desertion.

The first man to be hanged was Captain Brixy, and he remained as defiant as ever, jumping nimbly up the steps to the gallows and tying the noose himself. He showed no remorse and made no confession before stepping off the platform and twisting at the end of the taught rope until he choked to death.

The second man was more remorseful in the end. He spoke to the crowd, admitting that he had gone astray and lived a life of sin, although he did not address the specific crime of murder. Still, he refused to implicate any specific culprit in the murder at hand.

The third man to suffer the feel of the rope was poor Mr. Levett. It was not until that last minute that one of the officials stepped in to announce that the man had been granted a reprieve by the magistrates.

The late-arriving announcement nearly rendered the dramatic act moot, as the man nearly expired from fear during the display. [3]

A Foul Murder?

One day in 1744 the city received notice that a "foul Murder" had taken place by a man working on a trading boat somewhere between Savannah and Augusta. The man was accused of "Stabbing his Comrade with a Knife," and the message came as a request that Savannah officials apprehend the man before he disappeared — even though the notice had arrived by letter, along with the written testimonies.

The culprit was apprehended and was put into the Savannah jail to await his trial. Considering Savannah's reputation for harsh punishments for minor infractions, the outcome of this case may come as a surprise. When the man "came upon his Tryal," it was discovered that "the deceased was the Aggressor, and had fallen upon him and beat him Cruelly." The dead man had "followed him to his Hutt [and] renewd his Blows" and received a fatal blow to the head in an act of self-defense. The man was found innocent and set free. What is more surprising is that this man was a free African. It was not common for Savannah juries and the magistrates to show mercy, but they did for this man, whose name is lost to history.[4]

8

EVERYDAY LIFE AND PUBLIC PLACES

Walking about in the early days of Savannah was not that much different from a stroll today, when it comes to jobs, weather, and pests. "We are pestered by a little fly they call a Sand fly," one man wrote. "I have seen it in England about the Horse dung. But every insect here is stronger than in England." The man went on to say that the ants were a half an inch long and the alligators lurked by the side of the rivers, menacing the town folk, although they believed, at first, that the lizard-beasts were not able to reach high ground. As men labored to clear the land, they were reminded that the land was a "Harbour for snakes and vermin."[1]

The town was much smaller, of course, and the perimeter was clearly marked so that no one would wander too far away from civilization and fall prey to the many dangers that lurked in the woods. The Yamacraw land was marked on the East end by a blazed line exhibiting a red cross, while a road to the South marked the bottom end of town. The Western edge stopped at Indian Creek, while the Savannah River marked the northernmost line. No man was allowed to cut down trees outside the town. The sandy streets would likely smell of freshly-sawn wood and ocean breeze.

We can see what items were considered essential to a fledgling town, by the list of necessities compiled for a group who planned to settle further up the Savannah River. Settlers asked for a sand hour glass, pewter containers for drinking beer, one bell for ringing people to church or to call people to public work, flannel for night shirts, great guns for defense, and lanterns.

Streets and Buildings

The first houses in Savannah were one-story structures, but each house had an attic or "cock loft" above, large enough to place two beds. The houses may have varied in construction, but they had room to build three rooms below: typically one large and two small. The floors were made of wooden boards. Each of the early houses had a fenced yard measuring twenty yards by thirty.

Other buildings constructed right away were the bake house, the courthouse, the house for strangers, and the Trustees' Store, where settlers could get food, clothes, tools, and building supplies to get them through the first years.[2]

The Savannah Store

The Trustees' store was a colonial version of a super store: it was a supply house stocked with everything from molasses to muskets. Included in the settlement contracts for many colonists was a certain amount of store credit, so colonists could visit the establishment any time they were short on supplies. Some colonists increased their store credit through bartering with their own products and skills, supplying additional items for the town's consumption, like produce, hand-made tools, candles, and even wigs.

While the store was, for a long period of time, managed by Thomas Causton, inside this store, two domestic servants would be toiling away, stacking goods, serving customers, and counting stock. One incident from 1737 gives us a glimpse into the store operations.

Mr. and Mrs. John Desborough visited the store for a bag of molasses. They were shocked to see that the servant preparing this order spilled some of the molasses "out of his Bag and into a puddle of water." Mr. Desborough watched as the servants scooped up the molasses from the ground and put it in the bag again. The Desboroughs went straight to Bailiff Causton to complain of the matter. Causton investigated and learned that, while it was true that a bit of molasses had spilled, it had dripped onto a clean place. The customers had overreacted and "called them Thieves, Cheats, and Rogues."

Causton replaced the molasses and reprimanded his servants, but told Mr. Desborough that "if he desired to have any goods from ye Store, he must come for 'em in a quiet manner."[3]

The store was essential for the colony's survival, and the inventory provides a glimpse of everyday needs in the early eighteenth century. Food items available in the store included dried apples, smoked beef, coffee, dried tongues, deer suet, oats, wheat, and butter. Other items found at the store were tools for building and cutting trees, spices, cloth, and an assortment of other items that can be found in the inventory list.[4]

122 pounds of butter	20 pounds of honey
1008 long pipes	Breeches
72 short pipes	Waistcoats
Box of cut tobacco	Box locks
6 two-hour timer glass	10 frocks with red sleeves
8 one-hour timer glass	100 pair ear bobs
22 muskets	13 necklaces
1095 pounds smoked beef	1 pair saddle pistols
478 pounds of candles	11 pairs of children's shoes
1 pair of drumsticks	3 belly bands for felons
5 iron candlesticks	1 fireman's axe
37 gallons lamp oil	7 wooden compasses
396 pounds of coffee	38 pounds deer suet
92 pounds of brown sugar	33 brass handled cutlasses
590 flints	6 long swords
6 large three-pronged forks	67 dried tongues
21 pairs of coffin handles	1 bushel dried apples
2 hunting horns	1 case of surgeon's instruments
19 beaver hats	10 hats
148 pair worsted stockings	4 fishing sea nets
40 oars	102 wall hooks

The Trustees' Store was located in a trust house in Johnson Square. Some of the more interesting items in the store were deer suet, which could be used for flavoring a pot of vegetables, but it could also be used to soften leather. The store carried every item that colonists could need, and it appears that the town constable would have to pay a visit to the store if he were in need of more belly bands to secure his prisoners. Jewelry is another interesting item listed in the store inventory. A suitor could visit the store to find ear bobs or a necklace for his love interest, possibly wedged between the beaver hats and hunting horns.

Food and Drink

While there were some hungry times in Colonial Savannah, starvation was not a major problem in town. From its earliest days, the town was gifted with livestock from several benefactors, and these animals were placed in the woods, either in pens or in free herds, marked and left to graze in the swamps. Additionally, produce seems to have been available in sufficient quantities from the gardens that dotted the landscape. Every settler was required to improve their country lands, and that included a plot of land for growing a garden. There were orange trees, cabbage plants, turnips, carrots, and spinach.[5]

Cattle or pigs would be brought into town a few at a time and slaughtered. Fresh meat would be available briefly, but any meat that wasn't consumed right away would be salted and barreled. A typical midday meal in the early days was a plate of meat, and it was sometimes accompanied by cabbage or carrots and bread.[6] The townsfolk did not fashion their food into sandwiches, though. It would be another twenty years before the Earl of Sandwich placed his meat between two slices of bread and started a new food craze.

Breakfast customs have changed drastically over the centuries, and varied from place to place. It appears that breakfast in Savannah in the 1730s consisted mainly of meat and fish. There are a few accounts of William Stephens enjoying plates of meat for breakfast with friends. Samuel Eveleigh also mentioned a friendly breakfast in May of 1735. He was fed a plate of fried catfish and perch, as well as a bit of cold pork. He enjoyed rum punch to drink with the meal, and wine afterward.

By far, the drink of choice in Savannah was rum punch. In fact, by one account, it was a universal opinion that "rum punch is very wholesome, and would contribute to the health of the people." That idea may have come from the fact that citrus was a lifesaver for English sailors on long voyages, and a typical Savannah rum punch consisted of rum, lime juice, sugar, and a sprinkle of nutmeg. Any time there was a party, or a reason to be cordial with company, rum punch was involved. In fact, rum punch was popular throughout the English colonies, and decades later, it would be mentioned as a favored drink among the Founding Fathers.

Sadly, some settlers may have loved the drink a bit too much. Oglethorpe complained that some of the people in town were inclined to trade away their food provisions "for a little rum punch."[7]

Pubs and Inns

A visitor or newcomer might find a place to rest his head at the House for Strangers in Savannah, which was located near the public bakery in Johnson Square. This oddly named structure would serve as a primitive hotel, where a newcomer or a visitor could find temporary lodging, as well as a hot meal and some close company. For the first year or so, when the death rate was high enough to keep many wary new settlers away, the town's growth was slow, so the House for Strangers had few occupants. But after a time, merchant ships began to bring new settlers to the town. At one point, the House for Strangers must have been booked at full capacity, as one woman complained that she was put up in a private house instead of proper lodging, where she was "stuffed with all sorts."[8]

Once the town was more established, a handful of enterprising freeholders began to build extra rooms onto their existing properties to make room for visitors. Four licenses were granted each year in Savannah for public houses, or pubs, where visitors could find lodging. Of course, it wasn't long before these establishments became rowdy centers for plots, gossip, dancing, rendezvous, and illegal drinking, so this was not exactly a luxurious option for the newcomer. In fact, one man was traumatized by his stay, as he soon learned that life in the swampy wilds of Savannah was nothing like life on the London streets, as awful as they might have been. "They put me in a little house so out of repair and my bed lying on the floor I was afraid to lye or stay in the house after I'd catch'd 2 young Rattle Snakes coming in the door."[9] As if the snakes weren't enough to rattle the poor man, he later found two toads in his bed.

Gallows

There were hangings in colonial Georgia, to be sure, but there was not a specific place at the courthouse where a permanent gallows stood, as many believe. A gallows could be constructed simply for a single purpose, or it could be constructed more elaborately, for multiple uses. It appears that Savannah used both methods. When three sailors were to be hanged for a murder that occurred in the Savannah harbor, the order that came from the magistrates stated "that a Gallows should be erected on the Bluff... near the water, as near as we could judge opposite to the place where the Sloop lay, when this Murder was committed."[10]

That hanging place was intentional, it is clear, designed so that the murderers could look out upon the water where their deed had been committed. In fact, that was a practice known in England when dealing with pirates. But there is indication that it was also customary to hold the morbid show (which it was to the residents) outside the town perimeter when the condemned was a regular, common criminal. When two murderers were executed in 1741, the gallows was constructed "at the ordinary place of execution, a little Way out of Town."[11]

So what would a spectator see when attending a hanging in the early 1700s? There would be an executioner, a drummer to summon the community to observe and to accompany the official announcement of the sentence, a big crowd, and a few officials. Every condemned person would have the chance to ask for forgiveness and pray for peace in the afterlife before the deed was done. The death would have been a long and drawn out spectacle, since the merciful "drop" floor, which offered a quick death and a snap of a spinal cord, was not introduced until 1760. A hanging in early Savannah would be a long process, whereby the condemned person would walk off a plank and slowly die of strangulation, kicking and twitching as onlookers marveled. Once the condemned person was dead, the body would be thrown into a cart and carried to a burial place.

Daily Bread and Baking

While meandering down Bull Street, it would have been difficult to resist the aroma wafting from the town bakery, where town folk could find bread and other delights. Inside the bake house would be a variety of goods, as well as an assortment of spices and herbs that hung from the ceiling to dry. A visitor from Charleston noted that Savannah boasted "a glorious oven" made of brick that convinces any traveler that "there is no want of good Bread." Savannah must have enjoyed a good share of baked goods in those first few years, as most every merchant ship entering the river in those days contained a mix of flour, biscuits, and molasses.

Bread baking was so important to the colony that, in time, laws were passed to control the quality and the prices to "prevent evil" from bakers who might take advantage of their positions. Three types of bread were under scrutiny from public officials in the early days: white, wheat, and household bread were to be sold under specific guidelines. Household bread referred to the cheapest of the three; it was a type of whole grain bread "without the separation of either the fine flour or the coarse bran," and it is the type "agreeable enough for labourers."

The size of bread loaves would vary with the price of supplies, but for pricing purposes, the dimensions were very specific. A four penny loaf of white bread must be half the size of a household bread for the same price, while a four penny wheat loaf must be three quarters the size of the household bread. All loaves sold in the market had to have the initials of the baker impressed or carved into the top of the loaf. Any bread that didn't measure up to regulations would be seized and fed to the poor.[12]

Private Things

There are early depictions of the town of Savannah, and one of the things missing from the yards of early settlers, at least in the first sketches of town, is outhouses. But fear not, because colonials were not complete heathens. It was common for people in the 1730s to use chamber pots to do their colonial business. There is absolute evidence that chamber pots were in common use in colonial Savannah, because there were a few of these items listed in the inventory of the storehouse. One of the pots was made to use with a chair-like device called a "close stool." While it is true that the contents of these pots was often dumped out of windows into the streets of London, it's not likely that this was the practice in Savannah. Pots would have been emptied into holes in back gardens, or (perhaps) a community pit dug for this purpose.[13]

Backyard privies did appear over the next few decades. In 1767 the Grand Jury of Savannah complained that "The Beadle of this Town" was on notice "for neglecting to keep the streets clean, and for neglecting to inspect the necessary houses, many of which are very offensive."[14]

9

THE DRINKING TIME

To fully understand the enduring love for drinking in Savannah, we need to go back to the earliest days to understand how the romance started. Long before Savannah was settled by a group of Londoners, the city of London had been experiencing a serious drinking problem. Like with many societal ills, the root of the drinking problem falls with government officials and their meddling.

A few decades before Savannah was settled, the English government had decided to make alcohol dirt cheap. This wasn't their main goal, of course, but it was the result of a scheme. In reality, they promoted the distilling of gin as a scheme to drum up grain sales and support local farmers. But the ultimate outcome was that alcohol became as cheap as water, some said, and by 1730, at least seven thousand gin shops operated in London, alone. The free flow of the toxic brew led to widespread moral decay and chaos. Children were abandoned, families were ruined, and livelihoods were lost-just at the time that the Savannah settlers were swept up from the streets and pushed out to sea by the gentle wind.

Having spilled out of London at the very height of the gin

craze, Savannah's settlers were quite familiar with the jolly, numbing effects of alcohol—but in Savannah, the free-flowing beverage was rum. Looking around, William Stephens would report that "private Rum-Shops had become as common among the People, in Proportion, as Gin-Shops formerly at London." Yes, it's true that one of the intentions of the Georgia Trustees had been to outlaw rum in Savannah, but that goal was never quite realized. All over town, pubs and private houses were selling rum, despite official policies —and town officials were joining right in on the drinking.

It's no surprise, since the people drank rum punch for breakfast and beer at night. There seemed to be an occasion to drink at every hour of the day. Poor old Oglethorpe was beside himself, complaining after a few months that his chosen people had grown more fond of drink and less inter-ested in improving their land, which (he believed) led to untimely deaths. He wasn't the only one to suggest that the frequent deaths in Savannah resulted from rum drinking. In 1737, Thomas Causton was first bailiff when he reported that a Mr. Morrison had died, "probably proceeded from a disor-derly course of life, being much addicted to Drinking." Savan-nah's reputation reached other lands, as well, as revealed in a report that circulated shortly after Savannah was established: *The South Carolina Gazette* reported in 1733, only a few months after the first passengers stepped forth on Savannah soil, that "Some of the [Savannah] People having privately drank too freely of Rum are Dead."[1]

Dead Drunk

In the first few years on Savannah soil, the settlement's population declined sharply, and rum was often blamed for a shocking string of deaths. It was simply impossible to keep rum out of the Savannah town. Rum sellers could sneak up the tidal creeks into the edge of town in the dark of night and make a quick sale to the eager colonists. In fact, one of Oglethorpe's biggest frustrations was that his former translator, Mary Musgrove, had set up a shop for selling rum right across the river. But on Savannah soil, the drink was officially deemed off limits. Not only were settlers forbidden to drink it, they were also forbidden to manufacture and trade it. But this declaration only led to more troubles. It became increasingly clear to Savannahians that Charleston enjoyed an advantage when it came to vital trade with Native Americans —and drunken English people—because it was perfectly legal for people in South Carolina to sell rum.[2]

Before long, Savannah streets looked a lot like the streets of London, with drunks galore. By the end of the first year, twenty-nine of Savannah's original one hundred plus colonists had died. In fact, the drink-related deaths came so quickly that the town had to stop marking the occasions with ceremony. At first, every death was honored with a gun shot and a ringing of the bell. That had to stop after a while, because people became traumatized by hearing the bells and shots multiple times a day.[3]

The Dancing Doctor

It was essential that the settlers get along with the Yamacraw people, a small band of the Lower Creek Nation, who lived in a nearby village. And relations were quite good, with the two groups exchanging gifts and making friendly gestures. At one point, several Yamacraw men provided an interesting performance for the settlers, one that involved a ritual dance with feathered spears, rattles, and drums. What a fascinating sight that must have been to the former city dwellers. It was all good fun until things turned very serious, late in the night. It

seemed that one particularly valuable member of the settlement, an apothecary named Lyons—one of the few men of
medicine—had disappeared. An alarm was called, a search
group was gathered, and torches were lit.

The nearby woods provided no answers. Despite their
calls and desperate attempts, there was no sign of Dr. Lyons.
At this point, the settlers were still living in tents along the
bank of the Savannah River, so it would have been easy for a
person to wander off and fall into the river—or into the jaws
of a wild beast. The search continued, until one of the party
had an idea. Maybe they should wander over to the Yamacraw
village to see if the land's native inhabitants could help.

A few men from the search party would have seen the
glow of a campfire as they approached the small village. From
a distance, they would also have seen a movement around
the fire. To their horror, as they moved even closer, they
would have realized that the movement was their own
missing doctor, who was clutching feathers in each hand,
drunk out of his skull, attempting to mimic the Yamacraws'
earlier demonstration, while a few of the puzzled natives
looked on.

For Oglethorpe, this would have been rather awkward.
He'd spent many days preparing formal exchanges and regi-
mented meetings with Yamacraw leaders. It was critical to
convey to the Native Americans the value of a civilized society, based on good European values, religion, and sobriety.
Imagine the chagrin as the search party realized that the
doctor had been setting their example. As swiftly as they
could, the men surrounded the merry doctor and ordered
him to return with them to the Savannah camp. He flat
refused, as he was, apparently, having the time of his life. The
men insisted, and eventually resorted to grabbing the man
and carrying his twisting, resisting body back home with all
the dignity they could muster.

With plenty of effort, they managed to get the doctor back to the camp and in his bed. It must have caused a stir, when the worried villagers saw the search party approaching, carrying their doctor. There must have been questions and whispers. Had the doctor nearly drowned? Had he wandered into the woods and lost his mind? Had he been attacked by an animal? However the scene unfolded, it is clear that the doctor was put to bed and bystanders were assured. All was well—until the doctor disappeared once again.

Once again, a small group of men strolled to the Yamacraw village, probably hoping they would not find the doctor there. But they did. There he was, dancing around the fire again, feathers in his clutches. Once again, he was carried back to the Savannah camp, where people kept a closer eye on the doctor.[4]

Drunken Assault

On a Tuesday evening, September 26, 1744, two indentured servants from the Wormsloe Plantation decided to
come into the town of Savannah for a little fun at a public
house. While out and about, they met up with a fellow who
would later prove to be a dangerous fellow and a "Stranger,
who had been observed for 2 or 3 days past to be idling about
town." The three men became well intoxicated, and, to no
surprise, "committed divers outrages."

During their drunken antics, the men got into an argu-
ment with one of the townsmen. Being a peaceable fellow, or
maybe realizing he was outnumbered, the gentleman went
quietly home.

This was not acceptable to the three drunken fellows, so
they decided to pay the man a visit. They went to his house,
and when he would not answer their calls, they forced open
his door. The terrified man attempted to stand up to his
aggressors, but one of them "knocked him down with a Brick
batt, and wounded him much." The commotion was noticed
by neighbors, who called out for the guard.

The drunken rascals were taken into custody and questioned by the night guard. It appeared that they had no
defense, except to say that they were drunk and didn't
remember what they had done. After a night in jail, the two
servants were released to Noble Jones, of Wormsloe. The
stranger was not released. A stranger who could not prove
any means of employment was considered a danger to the
town, so he was confined to close prison.[5]

10

TROUBLESOME SERVANTS

A s the colony grew, more waves of European servants would come to Georgia. Impoverished, demoralized citizens would approach the Board of Georgia Trustees and ask for permission to indenture themselves, essentially selling their freedom for a number of years in exchange for the potential to earn land and perhaps learn a new trade. During the indenture period, food and clothing would be provided. One farmer listed the items of clothing he bought for each servant yearly: four Osnaburg shirts (coarse muslin fabric shirts for working class), a hat and a cap, four pairs of shoes, a cloth jacket and breeches (finer dress), a blanket and a pair of Indian boots (high-top moccasins).[1]

The prospect of leaving all they knew and traveling so far away from home took a lot of time and money. It's unfortunate, then, that some travelers would be kicked off the ships before they ever made it to open sea. Sailing ships of the day would spend days and weeks in one place after passenger boarding, waiting for provisions or for favorable weather, tides, and winds. This provided enough time for some would-be Savannah servants to get themselves into deep trouble. Mr. Harman Verelst reported some misbehavior among a few passengers in 1735: "Our people are very healthy and very orderly; excepting two women servants ... whom I have set on shore for drinking and indecent behavior. I have also set on shore the Surgeon's servant (he having the itch)." The itch, it will come as no surprise, was a term used for genital scabies.[2]

Once in Savannah, many indentured servants would live outside the main town in villages where they could dwell among others of their nationality. In 1738, Mr. Bradley reported that "among those Germans under his Care, there was one Carpenter, which he expected would have been of good use in building Huts, etc. for his people." John Brownfield of Savannah noted in 1737 that a hut for an indentured servant was "generally built of round Poles and split Boards without any Frame Work and is commonly much smaller than a House."[3]

The Boy Who Lurked in Holes

It was common practice in colonial times for parents to send away their children if they were too poor to care for them, or for family and friends to take on the children of parents who passed away. In 1738, a young boy was sent to Savannah by a Reverend Mr. Smith, who had been fond of the young man's parents (although it is not known if the parents were living or dead). The boy was sent to the colony to live in servitude and earn his way toward freedom and land ownership. The boy, a young lad named Thomas Roberts, had ideas of his own when it came to his life in Savannah, and his plans did not involve a servants' duties.

After two years, Thomas had exhausted William Stephens, the first person to welcome him into his home.

Stephens complained that there was "no hope of reforming him under my instruction." The boy could not be deterred from running away into the woods and "lurking in holes" until a search party found him and took him home again. Once he'd met his wit's end with the boy, Stephens sent the lad to live with a master who lived a few miles outside of town, in hopes that the boy would behave better if there were no people to menace and rob. Alas, the second master was not able to rein in the boy, and he was returned to Stephens.

A well-meaning woman in Savannah heard of the wild boy and decided to try her hand at civilizing him. She "Cloathed him very neatly" and treated him kindly, but within weeks, the boy returned to his wicked ways. He ran away again, and was on the run for two weeks, "during all which time he was Thieving at Night & Laying close in his hiding Holes in the Day time." He was finally caught during his usual method of robbery:

 "By creeping under the House and in the Dead of the Night lifting up a Board of the Floor; & so getting in, took what he found for his purpose, either Eatables or such goods as he thought he could traffic with."[4]

The boy was put in the jail, where he stayed for three months, until the Savannah magistrates took mercy on him. They were convinced that young Thomas had, by that time, "smarted sufficiently to terrify him from the like again." There are no more indications of trouble from young Mr. Roberts.

All the President's Men and Women

William Stephens was the first president of the colony,

and the poor man suffered greatly when it came to securing good servants. "My two first women," he wrote, "proved to be errant whores." Once he rid himself of that shocking pair, he took on a woman who turned out to be pregnant. Soon, she was "so forward with child" that she was calling for a midwife.

His men servants turned out to be no better. "Generally they are a vile crew," he complained to the Trustees. One of them, a man named Anthony Binks who had come highly recommended, seemed promising at first. Alas, he "turned out to be an egregious Sot," and then a "downright villain." He allowed himself to be "seduced by a pack of Raskals, & learned in private to drink Rum ... as seen drunk by me before Breakfast time." Despite the best efforts by President Stephens, Binks failed to improve and eventually ran away. He was apprehended and jailed for a short time, before being sent to serve at the military post of Fort Frederica.[5]

The Red String Affair

It was January 10, 1734 when a ship was spotted limping off the shore of Tybee Island, Georgia. The guard ship that patrolled the area for Savannah investigated the floundering sloop, only to find that it was a damaged prison ship, loaded with forty Irish souls, including six women and thirty-four men. The ship, it was soon discovered, was initially bound for Jamaica, but it was turned away from fear of the prisoners. It then ran into bad weather, and was knocked off course and sustained so much damage from wind and waves that it was not able to sail. The ship floundered in the sea, and the occupants suffered greatly, prompting Oglethorpe to later say that they were suffering from "want of Victuals [and] many of them were dead."

It happened that the ship showed up at a time when

Savannah had suffered a great deal of loss, herself. Oglethorpe needed live bodies to help the colony survive, and these poor souls needed food and comfort, so a decision was made. Oglethorpe offered the ship's captain five pounds a head for the Irish folk, with a goal of setting them about the town to serve as servants for a number of years. He gave each of the widows in town a servant, and appointed one to each of the town magistrates. He appointed some to help construct a saw mill and some to work in the town garden. And soon the trouble commenced.

The Irish were not about to acquiesce easily into a life of servitude in Savannah. One man wrote that "they are constantly playing their Roguish tricks, Stealing from their Masters and carrying the goods to Some Others." He went on to say to General Oglethorpe that "the buying of these Convicts, was the worst Action you did whilst here." Another observer wrote that the Irish were "a Parcel of harden'd abandoned Wretches perfectly Skill'd in all manner of Villany," and that they had been cast out of Ireland "deemed too dangerous to be allowed to Stay there." Apparently, the rascally Irish constantly menaced and unnerved the Georgia settlers.[6]

The real trouble culminated one evening in March, when the town's quiet was interrupted by the peal of the alarm bell. Word spread quickly through the streets that a plot was underway to kill all of the occupants in town in an insurrection of Irish servants. The colony's freeholders armed themselves and took to the streets, and cannons were loaded and positioned on each side of town. The city recorder managed to capture one of the young women servants, and learned that the rumors were true. In an attempt to seize control, she said upon questioning, some of the Irish had agreed to rise up upon a signal, and anyone involved in the conspiracy was to wear a red string around the wrist for identification.

The days that followed this initial alarm remain murky in

the record books, and some have claimed that it was, in truth, a simple drunken scheme among a few men and women. However, during the investigation, many of the Irish servants were discovered wearing the telltale "red ribbon" on their wrists. There was not a mass murder, however. But there was a single murder possibly connected to the Red String Affair. It was that murder of William Wise, who had settled across the Savannah River on Hutchinson Island. It seems that Mr. Wise had made the ill-fated decision to take on two of the Irish prisoners.[7]

11

FISTICUFFS AND MUSKET SHOTS

S avannah was increasingly occupied by hardscrabble transplants from all over Europe, and it was only natural for the occasional squabble to break out on the sandy streets. Groups, cliques, and clubs were as common in the 1700s as they are today. Sometimes there were cultural clashes, sometimes there were disagreements and hard feelings, and sometimes there were just plain crazy moments.

The Gardner, the Goat, and the Goose

Since one of the goals of the Georgia Trustees was to establish a silk industry in the colony, it was also necessary for the town to establish a healthy garden with lots of leafy mulberry trees. Mr. Fitzwater was sent as the official gardener to help establish this industry. It was his job to grow the precious trees, as they were the one food that well-nourished silkworms cannot resist. Unfortunately, Mr. Fitzwater, as it turned out, wasn't a very good gardener.

He did try, but he met challenges.

One of his most frustrating challenges was the wandering goats that lived next door. They kept making holes in their fence and escaping to enjoy his mulberry plants. So one day, Mr. Fitzwater had quite enough of this problem, and he took it upon himself to shoot a goat that he discovered happily eating his plants.

His next door neighbor and goat proprietor was a Mr. Robert Williams. Upon hearing about the demise of his goat, Williams was enraged. Since there were no real law enforcers in the town, he decided to exact some revenge, and, specifically, to take out his frustrations on Mr. Fitzwater's geese. He set up camp in his yard (somewhere near the Trustee's Garden) and waited for Mr. Fitzwater's geese to stroll by. Sure enough, it wasn't long before an entire flock of geese strolled by, so Mr. Williams got busy and commenced on shooting the entire flock.

There was an unfortunate problem, in that, he got the wrong flock. The flock he shot up belonged to Mrs. Vanderplank, a different neighbor. She was a poor widow woman trying to make her way in Savannah, all alone. For Savannah gossips, this was a hilarious turn of events. Mr. Williams became the butt of jokes around the town and was soundly humiliated as the talk of the marketplace.

The ordeal did not end there. Fitzwater was so amused by the entire story that he decided to parade his own geese by Williams' house, in order to taunt the man. Sure enough, Williams opened fire again. This time around, Williams did not get off with mere humiliation. He was hauled off to jail for shooting a gun inside the town.[1]

Flying Drop Shot

One late summer day in 1740, William Stephens received a visit from a Mr. Noble Jones, another dignitary in the town. The two men met often, as they both had official duties to carry out, and they both had established homes in town, as well as in large plantations in the countryside. This visit started out like any other, but things took a turn as the visit concluded, and the two men bid farewell at the doorway. Jones had strolled a few yards down the street of Percival Ward, when a loud, booming sound startled the men.

A rattled Jones ran back to his friend's doorway, where Stephens had, moments earlier, been happily waving. Shaken, Jones reported that it was a ball from a musket, which he had heard "whiz very near him."

The two met chatted for a few minutes and gathered their senses until things quieted and Jones set off again. Stephens walked his friend to his gate, where he stood when another shot exploded, and this time Stephens heard the shot "clearly over my Head as I stood at the Gate of my Yard." By this time, a tythingman had arrived on the scene. He had been toiling in his smith's shop that sat on the back of Stephen's property, and one of the balls had lodged in the side of his shop.

The three now set off in the direction of the gunfire, and it wasn't long before the culprit was spotted, still standing with "loaden" gun in hand, "just within the Skirts of the town." Upon questioning, the man casually admitted to firing the shots, but stated that he was not shooting at any specific target. He was simply "diverting himself with his Gun." According to Stephens, "When we asked whether he thought it was a reasonable diversion or not, to stand without the town and fire a ball into it, leveling his piece directly: He had nothing to say more, than that he did not mean any Harm."

Not greatly satisfied with the man's response, the officials seized the gun and had the man committed to jail. Upon inquiry, they found that the culprit was an indentured servant to a Scotsman who was not the least bit fond of Mr. Stephens. While some people in town suspected that foul play was intended, Stephens refused to admit this was a sinister scheme. "I am unwilling to think he had a particular and impersonal Antipathy toward me ... to destroy a man in cold blood, who had never injured him, and hardly knew him."

The Scotsman later appeared to have settled in Charleston, with no plans to return to Savannah.[2]

Them Scotch Sons of Bitches

Savannah was a multicultural city, even in her earliest years. There was a significant number of Scottish occupants, and they tended to be a proud, insular group. One afternoon in 1737, a millwright named James Smith approached First Bailiff Causton to claim that a Scotsman named Stirling had just beaten him with no provocation, whatsoever. Causton sent for Stirling to question him on the incident, for this was a possible case of criminal assault. When Stirling came willingly to answer the accusation, he had a very different story.

The incident started when Stirling and a small cluster of fellow Scotsmen were amusing themselves with an afternoon stroll, walking up and down Bull Street, laughing and chatting and having a fine time. As they approached the river end of Bull Street, they saw a group of millwrights "sitting on a piece of Timber by the waterside." One of the men, the complainer in this case, lifted a stick and pointed it in the direction of the Scots, clearly gesturing as if to fire a gun in their direction. Mr. Stirling didn't appreciate the gesture, and his compatriots felt the same. They approached Smith and his fellow millwrights to ask the meaning of Smith's actions.

Smith, likely emboldened by the size of his own group of friends, was not about to be intimidated, so he claimed he "did not fear him," for he was only a Scotsman. He held up the stick again, in a threatening manner. With that, Stirling took the stick away from Smith and "beat him, & bruised his Shoulder."

Stirling explained that this was not the first encounter between the Scotsmen and the millwrights. The previous evening, the men had also exchanged heated words, much in the same manner. The Scotsmen were strolling up and down Bull Street when Smith had said, loud enough for all to hear, that "if ye Devil was to cast his net" in the street, "what a parcel of Scotsmen he would catch."

While both sides seemed to be in the wrong, Causton was inclined to rule on the side of the Smith, the millwright, because he was a young and industrious man. Stirling was ordered to appear at the next court.

Unfortunately, Smith could not leave well enough alone.

A half hour after the dispute should have been settled, two town officials were walking along Bull Street when they saw the same group of millwrights, still positioned at the riverside, and this time another of the group was spouting off loudly. This man was wielding a hammer and, once again, cursing the Scots. The officials overheard the man calling out that "If he could have his will, he would knock them Scotch sons of bitches brains out." To the town officials, these did not appear to be the actions of innocent, respectable young men. They apprehended the clearly drunken, hammer-wielding man, and escorted *him* to meet the bailiff. It was now becoming clear to Causton that both sides shared the blame of this quarrel. This time, he sent the rowdy mill-wright to sober up while confined in the stocks, where he could contemplate his unbecoming behavior. The Scotsmen seemed to be pleased with this outcome, and the trouble subsided—at least for the day.[3]

Assault & Scandalous Words

It was soon after the Scotsmen's trouble, at very next meeting of court, when three women appeared before the bailiffs. The wives of Joseph Simons, Joseph Pavay, and Thomas Beale came forward to settle a squabble that had, apparently, played out on the Savannah streets. A warrant had been issued for "assault & scandalous words committed and spoken by Simons on Pavay."

Having no lawyers in Savannah at the time, the three women were required to provide testimony for themselves, but it appeared that the women became so heated in their claims and exchanges that the poor bailiffs could not make any sense of their words. "They were too warm to give any intelligible account of the matter," Thomas Causton claimed in his diary, "I therefore told 'em (after much noise) that as to assault, they must call a witness to prove it." As for the scandalous language, Causton explained that his hands were tied, since this was a government court and not an ecclesiastical one. Interestingly, as he scolded the squabbling women, Causton reminded them that "common disturbers," if men, might be fined, "but women might be ducked."

With this, Causton recommended that the women drop the issue and make up. They did not. Finally, after much noisemaking, a new witness stepped forward. Mrs. Vanderplank spoke up on behalf of Mrs. Pavay to say that she had, indeed, been assaulted by Mrs. Simons. Causton accepted that testimony and required that Simons appear at the next court to answer for her behavior.[4]

12

SCOOPS, GOSSIP, AND SCANDALS

I n a time when any and all information can be broadcast
from one edge of the earth to the other in a blink of an
eye, it is difficult to image how word got around in a
colonial settlement, especially one situated far south of the
larger colonies of the North, where the first colonial newspapers were still in infancy. Imagine the difficulty of walking
across town in Savannah's summer heat (or violent storms)
to exchange small talk with a friend, or waiting months on
end for a letter from a loved one in England. But clear
communication is vital to the survival of any community, so
Savannah's first inhabitants had to come up with a way to
spread word far and wide, and sometimes urgently.

The City Bell

One of the very first contraptions to touch Savannah soil
was a large crane that was placed at the top of the bluff of the
Savannah River, near the place where the first large tents
were erected. Before the town's first citizens ever arrived,
General Oglethorpe and an advance party prepared the

landing area by building steps for the ship passengers and placing the crane on the top of the bluff. The crane was necessary to hoist up all of the goods, tools, and materials needed to build the settlement. But the crane also served as a center of communication, as it was used to hang the first city bell.

In early days, a community bell served many purposes. The peal of a bell was used to sound an alarm, to issue a warning, to call a meeting, to indicate the start or finish of market time, to wake the citizens, or to call attention to anything at all. It's no wonder that the erection of a bell was one of the first official actions in the fledgling colony, as the settlement was certainly surrounded by unknown dangers. This first city bell would surely provide a sense of security, but not surprisingly, it also provided an opportunity for mischief. After a time, the city bell was moved to the town's first City Market. In 1763, "some evil-disposed persons ... have broke open the door to the market" and carried off the bell pole. Then, in 1767, the bandits struck again. This time, the whole town received a rude awakening when "the lock of the belfry in the publick market was broke open" and the "bell was rung at an unseasonable time of night, to the great surprise of the inhabitants." A reward was offered for the discovery of the offenders, but there's no record of the culprits being caught.[1]

The Courthouse Post

There are many references to a message post in the court-house garden, but the post for hanging messages *may* have been the whipping post, serving a double duty. Nonetheless, colonists sometimes used handmade signs and attached them to the city post to spread gossip or make accusations of others.

One local squabble demonstrates the use of the post for making public accusations. It was common in 1733 for the local militia to carry out drills to make sure they were ever ready for an attack from the Spanish, who threatened on a constant basis. During a muster in Johnson Square, Mr. Thomas Gaspen was greatly offended when Mr. Joseph Fitzwater had the audacity to claim the senior post—he being a junior officer. To show his displeasure, Gaspen challenged Fitzwater to a duel "by Point of Sword."

The duel was to happen the next morning, but Mr. Fitzwater, "being willing to Sleep in a whole Skin" (wanting to save his own skin), failed to show up. Gaspen was so frustrated that he affixed a notice "at the standard Post" calling Fitzwater a coward. Gaspen later apologized to the Trustees by letter, for breaking the law they had established relating to duels.[2]

Sinister Minister Gossip

When it came to town gossip, the best places for settlers to hear the latest were the taverns and the city marketplace. One favorite topic was the clergy, for they never seemed to fail when it came to scandal, or at least accusations of scandal. Savannah simply did not enjoy very good luck with ministers—or ministers did not enjoy very good luck with Savannah. Men of the cloth were not always the most popular people in town, sometimes for good reason, but sometimes not.

One of the earliest ministers in town was Mr. Dixon, but people were not fond of him in this role. The trouble with him, according to several accounts, was that he was a "notorious drunk." After Mr. Dixon was relieved of his duties, Mr. Dyson took up the job for a spell, but he posed a new problem. According to the Earl of Egmont, Dyson was also a drunkard, but he also "marry's people at Savannah without License from the Magistrate in kitchens & cellars, some of whom have wives or husbands living."[3]

George Whitfield, famed evangelist and co-founder of Methodism, was not spared the tattle. Despite his legacy in Savannah, he was not always a popular man. He was accused by some in the colony of all sorts of scandalous things for a time, including affairs with men and women, alike. There were "Scandalous, False & Defamatory Tales and Reports, of and concerning" Whitfield, saying that he had an affair with "One Mr. Seward." For his part, Whitfield was not too dismayed by the gossip; instead, he claimed to be accustomed to scandal, as his good work often prompted resentment and frequent attacks.

Whitfield did have at least one supporter. William Stephens claimed that he was doing a good job in Savannah, but he was menaced in his work by the "Gay Gentry" in town who tended to be "Idle and Lazy," who practiced "open Lewdness, first making Whores of their female Servants; then cohabiting with them and their Bastards."[4]

Once George Whitfield had left Savannah, William Stephens was minding his business one day when he "heard Whispers" that a scandalous accusation was spreading through town, and the subject of the gossip was the current minister, William Norris. A woman of town posted that Norris was "lascivious and addicted to women." The word soon got around that Mr. Norris had been engaged in "criminal conversation" with his maid servant, and it was the kind of conversation that left women pregnant. Stephens, acting as president of the colony, called Norris in to answer to this scandal, and he vehemently denied being guilty of any such thing. The woman who had first accused the minister was arrested and questioned by the magistrates, who decided she was lying. They sentenced her to a few lashes at the whipping post, but Norris stepped in and heroically said that her apology would suffice.[5]

Nonetheless, the servant woman soon appeared about town, clearly large with child. This time she was the one called in for questioning in front of the magistrates. At first, the terrified young woman cleared Mr. Norris of all wrongdoing. Later on, when questioned again by another official in a more private situation, she claimed that Mr. Norris actually was the father.

Mr. Norris continued to deny the charges, and collected several statements from men of note who vouched for his character. The gossip continued, though, and the minister's reputation around town continued to spiral. Couples refused to allow him to marry them, and instead, stood to declare their marriage in open court. A dejected Mr. Norris soon left for London.[6]

13

PIRATES, SHIPWRECKS, AND SCALLAWAGS

I n a collection of ancient ordinances for Georgia, including the Colonial Acts of Georgia, there is a specific entry for dealing with pirates. The book of laws begins with an act for establishing a militia, and that law requires that every male from the ages of sixteen to sixty be prepared to protect the colony from attack. The men were required to appear for muster days six times a year, and they must come armed with "one Gun or Musquet fit for Service, one Cartridge Box with at least nine Cartridges filled with good Gun Powder and Ball that shall fit his Piece a Horn or Flask." The act goes on to detail how the men should dress, respond to an alarm, and behave if they detected danger and needed to alert the militia.

The act then addresses the danger that might come from the sea, and establishes a lawful right to respond from a potential invasion:

> "And Whereas several Parts of this province lying on the Sea Coast are exposed to the

Depredations of Pirates and Sea Rovers ... it Shall and may be lawful ... to disperse, suppress, kill, destroy, apprehend take or subdue any Pirate, Sea Rover, Indian, or other enemy."[1]

Colonial records go on to describe how the courts should handle the trial of these potential marauders, and it states that any property owned by these intruders could be seized and sold.

While many historians suggest that Savannah came along too late in history to have actual pirates running around on their streets, Savannah's eighteenth century officials would probably raise an eyebrow at that suggestion. This confusion stems from the fact that the profession of privateering came along right about the same time that Savannah was settled. Privateering was a legal form of piracy, whereby a private individual could secure a ship, a crew, and a license to seize the ship of a country's wartime enemy. Privateering was a money-making enterprise, as the privateering ship (if the privateers behaved) would deliver a seized ship and its content to the country that issued the license, and the captain and crew would all be rewarded with payment. The problem with this profession is that it quickly devolved right back into piracy. Some rascally privateers realized that they could make a lot more money if they misbehaved, and their behavior was sometimes outright pirate-like. The legends of pirates menacing Savannah comes from the privateering ships that would visit the town. Well into the nineteenth century, salty, devilish marauders would spill into the city and create havoc in the pubs and inns.

As for the town leadership, they didn't mince words when it came to calling a pirate a pirate. As late as 1819, officials were still using the term, when it was reported in Savannah that six pirates had escaped from the Savannah jail. There were thirteen men held in all, and they all conspired to fashion a rope from their bed sheets and break through a window. Six of the men succeeded before the guard noticed, and put an end to the deed. But those six made their way to a creek, stole a craft called the *Charming Patty*, and fled to the sea.[2]

Mutiny on the James

Sea passengers were at the mercy of cruel and criminal-minded crews. In 1733, a ship filled with Savannah-bound passengers and fitted with six guns was headed across the Atlantic when the "Fore-mast Men threatened to run away with the Ship, and mutinied against the Captain, Mate, and Passengers." They were near enough to Port Royal in South Carolina to signal for help, and a "Lieutenant Watts, with the garrison boat, went immediately on board, & reduced the Mutineers to Reason, putting the Ringleader of them, who had formerly been a Pirate, and taken the Benefit of the Act of Grace, into Irons."[3]

An Unlucky Crew

It was a few years before the first lighthouse was completed at Tybee Island to protect sailing ships as they neared the shallow shores of the Southeastern coast. As the first tower was under construction, a watchman was posted on the island to keep an eye out for approaching ships. Some ships would approach the shore and fire a signal canon as they waited for a pilot to board the vessel and navigate up the Savannah River. Other ships might lurk outside the shore for clandestine reasons, while others might limp toward Tybee's shore after suffering damage from weather or pirates. It was important to have a watchman there to ward off any sign of trouble, for citizens on shore as well as on board ships.

On February 27 1741, a large brigantine filled with provisions from New York had gone off course and wrecked near the mouth of the Savannah River. A few of the town's most wicked occupants hatched a dastardly plot, and made off for the location to see if they could get ahold of any floating loot that might be driven ashore.

Savannah officials, of course, were incensed at this notion, and declared that any boxes or goods washing up from this disaster should be handed over to the trustees. As it turned out, most of the flotsam passed by the island and floated ashore on the nearby Islands of St. Catherine and Sapelo.

Later that year, a watchman at Tybee Island spotted another ship. As he peered through his eyeglass, he saw a sail in the distance of a small ship appearing to be in distress. He went out to see if the crew was in trouble, and found the ship's top masts severely damaged. He boarded the ship and guided it safely into the river and brought three of the crew into Savannah.

The ship was now sitting vulnerable in the Savannah River and word got around Savannah that "Dealers in the Dark" were preparing a nighttime visit to the ship to "see what was to be had." One of the "sturdiest Tything-men" was sent to board the ship and was told to prevent "any Person whatever" from boarding in the night.

Little did Savannah's villains know that the crew of this ship, called the *Polly*, had already been through one pillaging, and had nearly lost their lives to a band of Spanish scalawags. While cruising near the coast of Virginia, the little ship had been chased down and boarded. The captors put half the crew in their ship and headed for Florida with both vessels. On the way, a dreadful storm struck and pummeled the boats, causing the two to be separated. The storm destroyed the masts and sails and left the *Polly* drifting off the coast of Georgia.

The Spaniards managed to abandon the damaged vessel and board their longboat to set off for St. Augustine. Before they left, they "barbarously bored a Hole through the Bottom" in an attempt to kill the passengers and destroy the evidence. Fortunately, one of the more humanitarian of the Spaniards secretly warned one of the passengers before setting off, so the hole was spotted and plugged before the ship filled with water. It was the good fortune of the prisoners that the Tybee watchman spotted the boat languishing in the sea.[4]

Deserted Crew

Also in 1741, a Captain Howland and nine of his crew were discovered in a starving, miserable condition on Little Tybee Island. They were discovered in a small vessel floating off shore, their clothes tattered and spirits in a very low state. They were carried into Savannah where they were fed, and they told the following tale.

They were somewhere near Havana when they were attacked by pirates and put ashore on a deserted island. They were there for weeks, until one of them spotted an abandoned canoe in a stream. They made two paddles out of branches and took the canoe out to sea where they spied a small vessel coming straight for them.

Fearful of being killed, they pulled ashore again, and cut a stout club for each of them. They took their canoe out again and pulled alongside the vessel, which had only three men on board. They put the sailors into the canoe and seized the boat, but found only four biscuits to share between them. They made off to sea again, heading north to avoid any Spaniards, where they suffered many hardships.

They once settled on another island and were starved so much that they soaked a cow's hide in water and ate it whole. They set off again and finally settled on Little Tybee, where they collapsed and were later saved by the good graces of Savannah's citizens.[5]

"Damned Me for an American Rascal"

Savannah endured mistreatment from the piratical types for a good century after settlement, so it is only proper, when speaking of pirates, to venture beyond the colonial years. In 1801, an unfortunate gentleman named Captain Lancelot Davison embarked from Savannah on the ship, *Louisa*. When he was well out to sea, he realized that he had a leak, as he discovered five feet of water in the hold. He ordered the pumps to run constantly, and in a valiant attempt, threw one third of his cargo overboard "to keep the ship up." He managed to find the greatest leak, and attempted to plug it by nailing blankets and tarpaulins over the crack.

It was not long after this effort, that the ship "was boarded by a French pirate." The pirate examined the near-empty, sinking ship and soon realized that there was little to steal. The frustrated pirate "began to rob me of my provisions," the captain reported. The pirate "unrove all the rigging that was worth his trouble, took all the spare rigging that I had, marline, spun yarn, housing, Hambro line, pump leather, lanterns, speaking trumpet, time glasses, and in fact everything he could see worth his notice."

In an attempt to reason with the man, the captain reminded the scoundrel of the treaty that existed between France and America. Upon that, the pirate "damned me for an American rascal, and told me if I had a good cargo of flour or rice all the treaties that they could make should not save me, and if I said one more word he would set the ship on fire."

Apparently, it wasn't enough to steal the man's possessions and threaten to leave him and his crew for dead on a
burning ship. Amused with himself, the pirate added insult
to injury by placing the captain's own speaking trumpet
against the poor man's ear. "He then ordered me to make
sail, and wished me a good voyage."[6]

14

FIRST NATIONS PROBLEMS

For the Georgia Trustees, the settlers, and all involved, one critical need was to establish a friendly, respectful relationship with the First Nations people living in the environs surrounding Savannah. This endeavor was successful for the most part. The Yamacraw settlement was very close by, and there were visits, mutual gifts, and declarations of respect from the earliest days, as many have noted in history books.

The Savannah colonists were fascinated by the native people, and they always watched in wonder at the occasional display of dancing and rituals. However, it would be wrong to say that the relationship between Savannah's settlers and the First Nations groups were always calm and drama free. There were several incidents and accidents that created tension between the white men and the natives to the land, and it would be fair to say that the thought of a sparking conflict between these groups was ever lurking beneath the surface.

Of course, nothing could incite the furies of men like a sex scandal.

Blanket Sex

Musgrove's trading post was located a short way up the Savannah River from the colony, and it was the site of many interactions between whites and the Creeks and Yamacraws. It was not a surprise to anybody, then, that some of the troubles between the Savannah settlers and the natives took place on those premises.

One day in the fall of 1734, there was a scandalous rendezvous between a man named Wiggon, a servant indentured to Musgrove, and a married woman from the Yamacraw Nation. While details are sketchy, one newspaper account from Boston reported that Wiggon gave the woman a gift of a blanket, and she entered his hut on the Musgrove property, and the two engaged in sex. Unfortunately, the affair was witnessed by two Yamacraw men, and they quickly reported what they had witnessed. News of the event traveled quickly, and it did not go over well, on either side of the Savannah.

It wasn't long before the woman's husband showed up at the Trustee's Store with a few of his brethren at his side, and the husband wielded a long stick. Attached to one end was the woman's hair and a piece of her ear (she was not killed). The men made it clear that the appropriate punishment for adultery was death. They wanted Wiggon, and they headed for Savannah town to collect him.

Savannah officials were in a bind. They quickly sent for Wiggon, but they could not, in good conscience, turn him over to be put to death for a sexual tryst. Additionally, officials knew that Wiggon had friends and, perhaps family, in Savannah. Allowing him to be tortured and put to death would likely stir up a frenzy and destroy any peace that might be accomplished by turning him over.

The Yamacraw men stayed until Wiggon was brought in, and watched as he was detained. Savannah officials made a display of putting the man in chains and locking him away in the logg-house. They promised the Yamacraw men that the offender would be tried soon, and that they could attend to bear witness and to make sure the trial was fair. The men were reluctant, but they did agree.

The dilemma that Savannah officials faced was apparent in a letter that Thomas Christie, Town Recorder, wrote to Oglethorpe, proposing the idea that Wiggon should be punished more harshly than law would normally allow. After all, there was plenty of wife swapping and husband hopping going on, so there was a precedent for punishment, but it was clear that the status quo would not do in this case. Christie believed that the survival of the colony and the lives of the Georgia settlers could be at stake if they didn't satisfy the offended men.

In the end, the trial took place with the Yamacraw men in attendance. Wiggon was sentenced to a severe public whipping on Bull Street, which the Native Americans were invited to witness. This seemed to ease the tension and satisfy the Yamacraw group. One of those in attendance was Skee, an important figure in the Yamacraw village as well as in Savannah.[1]

Lunatic Watson and the Murder of Skee

Around Savannah, it had long been suspected that one citizen, a Mr. Joseph Watson, was a lunatic. There were rumors that a woman from Charleston had driven him mad with her rejections. He was an Indian trader who frequented Mary Musgrove's store, although the two had fallen out after he accused her of being a witch. There was also the matter of shooting her through the arm, which would have turned out a lot worse if she hadn't overpowered him and wrestled the gun away.[2]

Nonetheless, he often hung out and drank heavily with the servants or the natives who came and went at Musgrove's. According to records, he "was so seldom Sober That it was hard to Guess that he was not Mad. He would be naked with the Indians, drunk with them, lye down with them, and sometimes pretend to Baptize them."

It was because of his odd behavior that no one took him very seriously when he boasted that he had drunk Skee to death. When Skee's stiff body was found in the cow pen, then, William Stephens tracked down Watson and interrogated him on the events that had led to the man's death. Watson was aloof, saying that Skee had been too weak to handle the hard drinking and boasted that "Skee was dead & he alive."

Once again, the town was on full alert and nervous with the possibility of revenge. Stephens reminded Watson that he would not find the situation so amusing when Skee's friends and family heard of his talk, since they would view the death as a murder that required retribution. And, sure enough, they did exactly that.

A friend of Skee's named Stitchee decided to take the law into his own hands and set off to kill Watson. He tracked him down, right back at Musgrove's trading post, conducting business as usual. Mary was there when Stitchee and friends approached, and realizing what was about to take place, Mary locked all the doors to the building. As the men banged on the door, Watson (at Mary's direction), fled through a window and made his escape.

Now the town had to deal with the fact that several Yamacraw members were, indeed, out for revenge. To add to this problem, was the fact that Savannah citizens went on the defense on Watson's behalf. It wasn't a real murder, so they couldn't stand by and watch the man be handed over for certain death. Stephens tried to persuade Watson to leave town, but he refused. The solution was to find a reason to lock up Mr. Watson. A grand jury was assembled, and Watson was convicted of a misdemeanor and locked within his own home, with doors and windows nailed shut, and held there for several years on the charge of lunacy.[3]

Shot Through a Hole

Violence against any of the Native Americans was strictly forbidden, and Stephens managed to avoid this as best as could be expected, but violence *between* those who gathered in Savannah was just as dangerous when it came to keeping the peace, but much more difficult to prevent.

One day, the town was visited by a small group of Cherokee, who insisted upon a meeting with Oglethorpe. This meeting would be granted, in all likelihood, but Oglethorpe was not in Savannah at the time. The Cherokee insisted on waiting for him to arrive, and let it be known that they expected lodging and food while they waited. These requests were granted, as most of their demands were under such circumstances, and the men were put up in a house.

As it turned out, the neighboring Creeks and the Cherokee did not get along. A group of Creeks came into town and "joined Company" with the Cherokee. The gathering of the two groups put the town on edge, but no one in the town had the authority to interfere.

The men seemed to be civil with one another, as it was reported that they met "without any Quarrel then arising." The peace did not last long, however, and it was soon apparent that the peaceful display was an act. One of the Creek quietly left the group and, at some point, "went out, and, putting his Gun thro a little hole in the Boards of the House, Shot one of the Cherokees into the Head, a little beneath the eye." The ball lodged in the man's head, but he did not immediately die.

The town surgeon treated the wounded man, and peace was somehow maintained, for the time being. But the incident sheds light on the tensions that swelled any time violence erupted among the First Nations—even when Savannah merely provided the setting.[4]

Creek Revenge

On the early morning of July 27, 1744 the battered, beaten body of a Creek man was discovered lying on the bank of the Savannah River on the north edge of town. Of course, this prompted a hasty investigation into the apparent murder, and it wasn't long before the story was revealed.

The day before, a normally peaceful group of Creek men came to town to visit one of the pubs and enjoy a night of drinking. While enjoying their festive night, they spied a "straggler" that they knew too well: he was another Creek man who had been "the Author of the death of one of their Relations." Among the Creeks, it was customary to take the life of a man who has killed a relative. As such, they fell upon him with fists and any weapons with "an Abundance of savage Treatment."

The men abused the body greatly before tossing it into the river. The inquiry revealed that there had been several townsfolk who witnessed the event, but "none dared to interpose, which would have turned their Vengeance on any that attempted it." Instead, the town officials arranged a hasty burial, and the chapter was closed.[5]

15

UNHAPPY ACCIDENTS

Diary-keeper and Savannah's colonial president, William Stephens, noted several tragic events that he called "unhappy accidents." These events illuminate the dangers of living in a time when even the most innocent situations could become deadly, and when the medical care, alone, could kill a person. As if the hostile elements and the creatures that lurked in the swamps weren't dangerous enough, a stumble in a doorstep could prove deadly, under some circumstances.

Bathing Disaster

It was June 22, 1741, when a young man's body washed up on the shore of the Savannah River. It wasn't a surprise to the townspeople, for this young man had been missing for several days, and there had been suspicion that the youth, Elliot Watson, had drowned. But that was not what led to the young man's tragic demise.

Despite the disapproval of older folks, many of the lads about town had taken up the irksome habit of washing themselves daily at a certain spot on the river, late in the day, once chores were completed. Even though he couldn't swim, Elliot had clearly met his end while refreshing himself in the cool water in the dusk of the day. His clothes had been found in the usual spot along the side of the river, along with an old boat that had been pulled ashore.

As the body was pulled from the water, however, it seemed that young Elliot had met a fate far more horrific than anyone had suspected. One of the boy's arms had been bitten off at the shoulder. Many concluded that the lad had been seized by a lurking alligator as he entered the water, and dragged into the depths of the murky Savannah water. It was a wonder, one man surmised "that we do not oftener hear of such calamities, those voracious Creatures, being too frequently lurking for their prey," while young people would not be "deterr'd from Bathing almost daily."[1]

It should be little wonder that the more mature citizens tended to shy away from refreshing themselves in the river. Instead, they likely would have washed their faces daily from a wash bowl and bathed monthly at best, by collecting water from the river or the town well and filling a single tub for the entire family to enjoy.

One thing was clear: there was to be no messing about with a small spring on the edge of town that must have been reserved for refreshment. It was declared that no person shall "Make any fires there or Make it a place to wash Cloaths." Anyone caught breaking this rule was to have his tubs and pots broken up and be prosecuted under law. Another such freshwater spring was located "about a Musquett shott from Thunderbolt fort."[2]

The more fortunate would use a wash ball to clean themselves. This luxury item was an early version of a ball of soap, and it was made by placing an ordinary lump of soap into a mortar and beating it to powder. It was mixed with rose water (for scent) and hair powder (for texture). Other scents could be added using oil of thyme and oil of caraway. Shortly after Savannah was settled, an unlucky fellow named Joshua Overend passed away, and his estate included a wash ball, a razor, and a damask nightgown.[3]

Guard Boat

In order to keep the town safe from incursions from Spanish or piratical sorts, city leaders established a corps of guard boats that would patrol around the coastal waterways and islands. These small sailing vessels would keep a keen eye in search of ill-intended visitors. It must have been a boring job, for the most part. Naturally, one way to counter the mind-numbing boredom of patrolling the same stretch of water for hours on end was drinking.

"This Evening happen'd another fatal Accident, which we had too many Instances of lately. One Davis belonging to Capt. Noble Jone's guard boat ... being grievously drunk, tumbled overboard; and maugre all the Endeavors of the Boasts Crew to save him, he sunk and was drowned."[4]

Unlucky Shot

A young man from the orphan house was bound as an apprentice to the apothecary in town, and one day the master sent the boy into the woods surrounding town for a bit of squirrel hunting. In an unlikely twist of fate, the boy spotted a squirrel in the very place and a moment in time when another hunter, a Mr. John Sellie, spotted the same squirrel from the opposite side. The two men aimed for the squirrel, but unknowing pointed their guns toward each other. The older man shot first, and "not Seeing the Lad ... unhappily threw a great Number of Shot into [the boy's] breast, Arms, Face, etc, wherewith he was so wounded that now lies in danger of his life." [5]

Riding in the Swamp

One of the best and finest houses of public entertainment and refreshment in Savannah in the year 1744 was owned by John Teasdale. Countless entries in the colonial records show that his pub was a popular watering hole, where Savannah's first citizens could always enjoy amusing company and enticing refreshments.

One day Mr. Teasdale was out in the woods driving home a group of horses (allowed to graze in the wild) when he rode "hastily against the Stump of a Tree." The poor man "broke his leg short off in the middle, so shattered, that the bone came thro [sic] the Skin." The injury was such that his life was in great danger. Oddly, the man's son had suffered a similar injury just a few weeks earlier. The boy had an "accidental misstep at the threshold of the house ... [and] fell much in the same manner, and broke the other leg, just in the same part as the former."[6]

Accident on the Wharf

It seems like many unhappy accidents in Savannah's early days involved a drinking spell, at some point. One Sunday afternoon during church time, another scout from the guard boats experienced a fateful accident, only this one happened in town.

He "laid himself down to Sleep" on the wharf, it being a mild and pleasant day, but he must have placed himself a little too close to the edge. At some point, he turned over in his sleep and "tumbled into the River, the tide being then up, and nobody near that could swim to catch him, he was drown'd." The record goes on to add that it was not known if he had been "dealing too freely with Rum," but it was likely, since most of the boatmen who patrolled the coast "being addicted to it."[7]

Capsized

Savannah has always enjoyed mild winters, with the loveliest weather days occasionally stretching into December, and starting again in February. One week, three men took advantage of the mild climate to travel from Fort Argyle, the outpost settled several miles up the Ogeechee River, to visit Savannah to collect a few supplies. On their way home, the men encountered a fitful sea, as their boat overturned in the waves of the sound at the mouth of the Great Ogeechee. With much difficulty, the men managed to swim to a marsh "where they were forlorn and helpless." In time, one of the men decided that their only chance for survival would be if he tried to make his way back across the Ogeechee and through the many swamps and creeks until he found help. He set off, "travelling over divers Marshes and Creeks," until he came upon a native in a small canoe. That man took him in and carried the exhausted soul to the nearest guard post. From there, a boat was dispatched, and a search was soon underway for the two men left stranded on a muddy marsh. A short time later, the two men were discovered, and they were all three carried safely back to Fort Argyle.[8]

16

SCIENCE AND BEASTS

To a great extent, people in the early 18th century were fascinated by science and the natural world. There was newfound respect for nature in the early years of the century, and a growing philosophy that mankind should live in harmony with God's creations. The colonists who started a new life in Savannah soon realized that changing continents and latitudes brought new wonders when it came to the natural world.

Deadly Lightening

One of the major differences that these English men and women experienced in their new Savannah home was a drastic change in weather. The heat was expected, for the most part, since the Londoners had been warned of the hot climate that existed in the lower part of North America. But the violent storms that came along with the climate came as a surprise.

One Sunday afternoon, the Widow Fitzwater sat at her kitchen table along with two grown children: a son and a daughter. The brother was a tythingman and the current jailor. The daughter was twenty years old. On this day, a violent thunderstorm storm had settled over the town, like many had before in the odd new place they called home. The storms that settlers experienced in young Savannah were quite different and much more robust than the showers they'd experienced in England. There was much talk of the storms and the violence they begat. At one point, a bolt of lightning struck the town's light pole, and it was broken in half. But that was nothing like the thunder and lightning experienced by the Fitzwater family that afternoon.

As the family sat at the table, a bolt of lightning came through the window and struck the young Miss Fitzwater dead on the spot. As if that was not enough for the family to endure, the lightening took out part of the house, as "the Plastering of the house shatter'd to Dust."[1]

The Beast in the Woods

A remarkable report appeared in December of 1740 that a young man encountered a ravenous wild beast while out hunting less than a mile outside the town. The beast's identity was unknown, but it had been spotted on a few occasions and was suspected of killing pigs, calves, and young cattle that ran loose in the woods. Some suggested it was a mongrel breed, a mix of the known bobcat and some other beast of prey, for it was much longer than the known wildcats in the vicinity, the tail, alone, appearing to be six feet in length.

The mysterious animal approached the boy, so he fired a shot, but it continued to charge at him. Luckily, the boy had a dog with him, who managed to keep the animal at bay until the lad loaded another ball. Reporting on the incident, William Stephens explained that "The people here call them

Tygers," but that identification was disputed because the head was much sharper than a tiger's. There were similarities, Stephens said: the teeth and talons seemed similar, but the color was also not right. The tiger was naturally striped, while this beast was chestnut brown in color.[2]

The Spectacle in the Sky

One night in 1744, an amazing sight appeared in the sky, and it captured the attention of Savannah's "star gazers" for months on end. The object was a great comet, and it was so bright that it could, at its brightest point, be seen in the daytime. Known as Comet de Chéseaux, the amazing celestial object also displayed multiple tails: by February, two tails were seen by Savannah onlookers, and by March, a huge fan of six tails was visible.

While comets were known to science at the time, the drama and sheer magnitude of this particular object may have mystified them. Now known as one of the five brightest comets of all time, Comet de Chéseaux delighted and amazed colonials until it faded again into the night sky.[3]

The First Midwife

Elizabeth Stanley, aged 35, and her husband Joseph, a stocking maker aged 45, arrived with the original settlers on the *Ship Ann*. Elizabeth was the public midwife, who would deliver all babies in the first several years of living in the new colony. In 1734, Elizabeth reported her activities to the Trustees.

"I think myself duty bound to acquaint you how my affairs stand in Savannah," she wrote. "I thank God I have discharged my duty, both to ye honorable Trustees, and to the people." Elizabeth reported that, of all the fifty-nine women she had "led," through childbirth, none had miscarried.

Elizabeth was concerned, as she wrote, that she might be followed in her trade by charlatans, claiming to know her field, which would be disastrous for the women in her community. She asked the Trustees to "Crush the way of all false pretenders in her way of practice." She had reason to believe that one such pretender had already cost a few lives. A Mrs. Coat of Ogeechee had attempted to lead two women through birth, but the second woman she tried had died and the horrible woman had left her infant behind her.[4]

Medical Treatments

In the 1730s, local medical care was primitive and often brutal. The Age of Enlightenment was barely dawning, and rural practitioners were rarely well trained. Bleeding was still commonplace, and it was practiced in Savannah with enthusiasm. William Stephens seemed to embrace the practice for all sorts of ills:

> An accident befell me this Day, which prevented my stirring abroad: sitting at my table in the morning writing, my Stool happened to slide, and falling across it, I so bruised my Side, that I was obliged to take away a little Blood.[5]

In 1736, one ship practitioner told of his accomplishments on a journey across the Atlantic, when he lost only one infant and one woman "aged upward of 60 who died of old age." There were mostly coughs and colds to deal with, he reported, and he attributed that to the change in weather and the lack of exercise. Some people did have pains in their limbs and swollen feet and legs, which he treated with a "strong purgative," commonly known today as a laxative.

Diarrhea was quite common on board ship, due to a number of unpleasant things people would consume, from spoiled food to dirty water. For this ailment, the doctor would give a drink of burnt Hatshorn (crushed antler) and laudanum (opium tincture). Other medicinal doses were made of spermaceti, barley liquor, and an emulsion of Indian corn. Of course, the doctor treated fevers with bleeding.[6]

17

DANCING AND ENTERTAINMENTS

One of the first accounts of adult dancing in Savannah is recorded as a celebration of General Oglethorpe's birthday in 1737, just a few years after settlement. The celebration lasted all day, starting with treats and wine drinking at Fort Savannah, the structure situated on the Eastern end of Bay Street. The day began at noon, with a thirteen gun salute to mark the occasion, and ended up in true Savannah style, at a tavern, when "those who could find them" brought partners for dancing. This would not have been a formal type of dance, with the stiff, ritualistic steps you might expect in an eighteenth century stately ball. Many of those in attendance of this celebration were the same constables and magistrates who routinely came to fisticuffs in the street, and they would have been more familiar with the country dances that were common in England.[1]

A tavern dance would have required a fiddler and a space large enough for couples to gather in groups to perform a series of familiar steps. In the early 1700s, many country dances required couples to line up in long rows, or "longways, for as many as will." If the inside of the tavern did not furnish the space for a long line, the festivities could have taken place outside, in the tavern garden. While it was most common for dances to take place in long rows, space or weather constraints could have required the dancers to gather in small circles or squares.

English people in the seventeenth and eighteenth centuries danced everywhere and often, so the dance steps would have been familiar to people of all classes. An instruction book was first published in 1651 and became so popular that it was published in at least fifteen later editions. Savannah's dancers would, no doubt, be familiar with ditties like "Puddings and Pies," "Johnny Cock Thy Beaver," or "Old Man is a Bed Full of Bones."

Some dances came with lyrics to be sung. A tavern dance would surely have included "Mr. Lane's Maggot," published in 1695 and widely known, which would have prompted a chorus of voices calling out the words:

Strike up Drowsie Gut Scrapers,

Gallants be ready

Each with his Lady …

I'll teach you all the dance.

Cast Off, Tom, behind Johnny

Do the same, Nanny,

Eyes are upon ye.[2]

Skits and Plays

Sometimes, dancing could be hazardous, as we can see from this episode in 1734: "Last night a quarrel happened between Mr. Edward Bush the tythingman and his guard, & some gentlemen who were dancing. Many blows were given, and

Dr. Patrick Telfair like to have had his arm cut off by Bush, with his dagger."[3]

Obviously, the tythingman did not approve of Dr. Telfair's dance. While it may seem like the authority was abusing his power, there's likely a lot missing in this report. The dancing was most likely, in reality, a public mockery of those in authority. One method of expressing political views in the 1730s was through satirical plays and skits, acted out in the streets or in pubs. In Savannah, Wright Square was the hub of social life in those early years, and the most likely spot where this mode of entertainment might have taken place. In 1739, William Stephens grumbled that "Pasquin began to appear again." The name (and the act of performing a pasquinade) refers to an unknown actor who disguises himself and appears in a public place to ridicule and lampoon public officials. Savannah had its own disguised actor, and William Stephens complained that he demonstrated "Savannah wit" and poked fun at "all Sorts of people" and "provided good entertainment to many." The actor had clearly hidden his identity, as Stephens moaned that the culprit "was not easy to discover."

Skittle Alleys and Other Diversions

Racing was a popular sport in Savannah's early days. There were foot races, horse races, and wrestling competitions. Along with these amusements, it is possible that colonists would take up the London amusement of head stand competitions, and competitions of walking on hands. Having come from London to a much warmer climate, the citizens would have continued the friendly competitions that took place in the Thames, like swimming and sailing races.

Target shooting was another activity that the town used to amuse themselves, and this activity often concluded with a pair of shoes or a hat as a prize to the best shooter. One such competition sprung up during a holiday celebration, when a group of merrymakers contributed to the purchase of a fine hat and set it up as a prize for the best target shot. After that game was over, they began rolling dice for the grand prize of a horse worth twelve pounds sterling. The same day, a roll of the dice could win the lucky victor a fine canoe. Others participated in a game of cricket in Wrights Square.[4]

One amusement that popped up early in the young settlement was the game of skittles. Within the first year or so, taverns opened, and with the tavern, you would find amusements, such as card games and skittle alleys. Closely related to the lawn game of bowls, skittles is an ancestor to the current game of bowling, and a skittle alley was the grandparent to the bowling alley.

Skittles games came in a variety of formats. It was sometimes played inside, and sometimes outside, in the garden area of a pub. The original game was played with nine pins, and was played in teams. Each team member would specialize in a "bowl" according to the arrangement of pins left standing. For example, if the first bowler knocks down all pins but the three on the left, the team would call upon the left side bowler to go next. There was no specific rotation to the order of bowlers.

Down the Road

During the first few decades, Savannah's fun and games were limited due to geography. Savannah was situated so far in the wild, that townsfolk had to rely on one another for entertainment. After all, a trip to and from Charleston, the nearest city, would take several days, at best. But a few decades later, transportation had improved with the building of roads and bridges, and this opened up an entirely new world to Savannah, and changed the way the little city laughed and played.

With improved roads, traveling entertainers began to journey up and down the coast, traveling in carts or on foot, bringing their acts from New York, through Virginia, down to Charleston and Savannah. Entertainers would apply to the city leaders for permission to set up a display or put on a show for several nights. One of the first to apply to Savannah's early city council was a wire dancer named Thomas Saxon. It's likely that Saxon did not travel alone; instead, he would work with a group of entertainers, both men and women. They would string up a high wire and perform tricks much like high wire acts we see today, although the performers were more clothed in those days.

Rembrandt Peale was a famous American artist, but in addition to painting, Peale was an entertainer. He ran a museum and seemed to be fascinated with wildlife. He developed his own traveling show in the late eighteenth century, and brought mastodon bones and a "learned goat" to Savannah to entertain the crowds. Learned goats and pigs traveled the country performing card tricks and other wonders.

Wax works, dramatic plays, and tumblers performed in Savannah. Wild, exotic animals were put on display, and a fascinating gadget called the magic lantern made an appearance around the turn of the century. This device was an early form of projector, involving a wooden box, a candle or an oil lantern, and slides that could be projected onto a large canvas. A news report from Augusta stated that the magic lantern slides on display there included lions, tigers, panthers, and other animals, all with moving eyes.

Perhaps the most unique show to appear in Savannah was the antipodean whirligig. This was a one man show, in which the man would climb on a table and spin around on the top of his head at a dizzying speed. News accounts claimed that the man could spin two hundred and fifty times per minute on his head.[5]

18

COLONIAL OCCUPATIONS

I t's hard to imagine the challenge of establishing a brand new town in the wilderness, and making sure to include all the elements and positions to ensure that the community could sustain itself. The planners did what they could to make sure that the Savannah's settlers possessed the skills necessary for the town's survival. One of the most enlightening ways to explore the occupations that existed in early Savannah is to examine the challenges they faced or the trouble they caused as they went about their daily lives.

Turner, the Runaway Carpenter

Carpentry work was, perhaps, the most important skill during Savannah's earliest days. The first few months after settlement, the entire community took part in clearing land and erecting buildings for shelter and comfort, so skilled workers would have provided critical expertise. Sadly, Mr. Turner, one of Savannah's prized carpenters ran into a bit of trouble. Times were hard in the early years, and many settlers went into debt, just trying to survive.

One Thursday morning in 1737, the magistrates executed an order for Turner's debt (most likely to the town store) to be collected by a tythingman. Things did not go smoothly. When the tythingman arrived, Turner and his wife "used him very roughly," using a few blows in the process, and sent him on his way. The man returned to the magistrates and reported his abuse. The furious officials issued a warrant for Turner's arrest.

Turner was one step ahead of the law. When officials arrived, he was nowhere to be found. It was soon discovered that Turner's friends had assisted him in a getaway. Turner first slipped off to the home of his neighbor, a gunsmith who was also a notorious "dealer of spirits." Apparently, Turner was known to hang out with a rather notorious crowd. He had been previously involved in skullduggery of other sorts, as he was an accomplice to Mr. Mellichamp in the counterfeiting scheme as well as the prostitute auction.

The neighbor and others in the gang arranged for a boat to provide a getaway into the swamps, but just as the boat was making its way through the creeks, it was spotted by a sentinel and Mr. Christie, the town recorder. Christie ordered the sentinel to fire upon the fugitives, but Turner and his friends taunted the pair, challenging the two to fire away. It was soon apparent that the scoundrels were drifting out of reach of the sentinel's firepower, and the frustrated Mr. Christie could only watch as the vessel sailed away, leaving the echo of laughter behind.[1]

Town Cryer

John Sallie was Savannah's cryer, and in this role, he filled several duties. For every cause tried in court, he would receive six pence, and each time he swore in a witness, he received two more. When attorneys were finally allowed to practice in courtrooms, they were obliged to pay the cryer one shilling each after each trial concluded.[2]

The cryer was also called upon to walk about the streets to announce the opening of court sessions, the arrival of a ship, the creation of a new law, and a hanging, among other things. The town cryer may have been accompanied by a drummer or a bell ringer, and he would begin his announcement with the words, "Oyez, oyez!" Once he had called out his news, he would post a paper copy of his announcement on the courthouse door.

The town cryer worked for the government, so he may have walked the streets to make sure no fires were left burning before he settled in. The man in this position also attended public hangings and called out the crime as well as the sentence to onlookers. He would assist the hangman with cutting down the dead person at the end of the rope. Because of his varied duties, the ability to read was an absolute must for this position, and a robust voice and a commanding stature were the other job requirements.

Candle Shop

Savannah's first candle maker arrived in the colony in 1733. The town's first chandler, Richard Ecles, stepped off a boat and established a trade that would light the nights for colonial Georgia until the oil lanterns and gas lighting rendered the occupation of tallow chandler obsolete. Poor Mr. Ecles was not to survive for long in the new and hostile Georgia environment, but he would be followed by others who set up shop on Savannah's earliest streets.

A curious person might smell a chandler's shop before stopping to gaze through its glazed windows. Tallow is an animal byproduct that would have been secured from the town's butcher in lumps of cow or sheep fat (not pig, as that fat is too soft for candle making). The fat was boiled in water and skimmed from the surface. That product is put through a sieve to remove lumps and impurities, and the resulting tallow would be melted again. The chandler would dip a wick into the tallow several times until a slender candle developed. Candles were hung in rows to dry and harden, so anyone walking by the chandler's shop might see rows of candles lining the edges of the room.

One surprising use for candles was timekeeping. In the earliest days, clocks were scarce. Candles could be constructed to burn for a certain amount of time, so Savannah's early courtrooms and business meetings may have been timed with a one-hour candle or a two-hour candle variety.[3]

The Blacksmith

Most every colonial town employed a blacksmith, as metalworking was one skill that was essential to any early society. Blacksmiths would make the essential horseshoes, of course, but they also made tools that *other* trades required, like hammers, sickles, and axes. Walking about Savannah in 1740, a visitor might hear the ordinary *clank, clank, clank* of the blacksmith's hammer, as the fellow carried out his ordinary work. On the other hand, Savannah's handyman might be observed fulfilling an unusual request, as this was the year that the city officials ordered the construction of a gibbet, or cage, to hold the body of an executed murderer.

After the murder at Fort Argyle, Savannah authorities asked the smith to build a cage (called a gibbet) to hold the dead body of the Spanish spy. They wanted a cage that "would be conspicuous to all who would pass to and fro." Once the cage was completed, it was placed on a ship, along with the body of the dead murderer, and carried to the Ossabaw Sound and hung up for all to see.[4]

Wigs and Shoes

No colonial town would be complete without a person to provide the wigs for men and women who found themselves in the highest level of Savannah's fledgling society. In the 1730s, a big wig was essential attire for, well, bigwigs.

The first peruke maker, the name for one who designed wigs, was James Willoughby, but the poor man lasted merely a year in the hostile environs of Savannah, dying sometime during the period knows as the drinking time. In his occupation, the wig maker would receive bundles of hair from animals or humans and sew them into a net base. Tools of his trade would include tongs, scissors, needles, thread, curling irons and flattening irons, as well as chemicals and dyes. Included in the colonial store was a bundle or "butt of hair," which likely was designated for perukes.

A subsequent wig maker was named James Carwell, and he was a man of questionable character, although he seemed to make a good living from his occupation. In 1734 he was paid 205 pounds of Georgia currency for his goods, but he promptly turned to the pubs for comfort. Records show he "made shift to turn them to wett and drunk them up." The man eventually became a jailor, but he was no good for that, either. He soon had a reputation for abusing prisoners, and was deemed a cruel man "of very bad character."[5]

Silk Worms and Murder

One of the primary goals of settling the colony of Savannah was to establish a silk industry. What many people don't realize, is that, in the early 1700, silk production was a deadly dangerous business, fraught with espionage, secrets, and murder. To understand why silk production was so important to the colony, it's important to know the background on England's silk producing ambitions.

It was 1717, when a young Englishman journeyed to Northern Italy to undertake what may well be the world's first industrial espionage mission. He was determined to unravel the mystery of silk production, which had long been a precious secret guarded closely by the Italian government. Through the 1600s, silk had emerged in Europe as a much-admired luxury item, worn only by the most wealthy and prestigious members of society. This young spy, named John Lombe, was an astute businessman, and he knew that cracking the secrets of silk production and bringing it to England could prove very lucrative.

Once in Italy, sources say Lombe wormed his way into a silk workshop one dark night armed with candles, pencils, and sketch pads, and made images of the spinning machines. His clandestine venture was a success; he managed to complete his mission and smuggle the drawings back to his England home of Derby—but he barely made it out of Italy alive. The officials caught wind of his antics, and sent out a warrant for his arrest. The penalty for his crime would have been death by hanging. Nonetheless, Lombe made it out of Italy in the nick of time and traveled back home, where he and his brother began setting up a working silk factory. But they made one deadly mistake.

There's much more to the silk industry than spinning the thread. Silk productions requires special knowledge about the care of silkworms and the delicate leaves they ate. Again, the expertise in this field could come only from Italy, so the men hired a few Italian women to help them establish their business. It wasn't long before Lombe was dead from slow poisoning.[6]

Lombe's death came in 1722, around the same time the Georgia Trustees plotted to establish a silk industry in the far colonies. Since the industry was still cloaked in secrecy and it required delicate, expert care, officials did the logical thing when they began setting up a silk factory in Savannah. They hired a few Italians to oversee the project.

At first, things worked out fairly well. The first order of business was to establish a thriving mulberry tree crop, and some of the first ships to Georgia carried young trees that would be planted in the Trustee's Garden. The process of growing and nurturing worms was the delicate part. Leaves had to be carefully gathered by hand, one by one, in a manner that would not bruise them, yet the worms were so voracious that leaf gathering was a constant process, carried out by young women and indentured servants who worked for the town. The leaves, once plucked, were only usable within the first forty-eight hours, and in that time, they had to be turned periodically. Leaf care and worm feeding was a full time, nonstop occupation.

Silkworm eggs were as delicate as the mulberry leaves. The eggs were kept in homes around Savannah in lined boxes, near the firesides to keep them warm. Once the worms began to hatch and grow, they were placed on racks and put under care of a rat-catcher, whose job it was to protect them from rodents, birds, and stray cats.

The first man to oversee this delicate operation was Paul Amatis, an Italian from the Piedmont region, bought in from Italy upon the first ship. Amatis would send for his brother, Nicholas, within a year, but he did not last long in the wilderness. Nicholas "proved to be an idle troublesome fellow & quitted the colony" within two years. It may have been tension from Britain's impinging in this precious Italian trade that sabotaged the venture from the start—but whatever was at the root of the problem, the Italians who came to Savannah were marked as difficult, uncooperative, and destructive to the entire venture. In fairness, Paul Amatis may have tried to make the silk business successful, but squabbles with the locals doomed the enterprise from the start.

One such incident was the result of more bickering about the oversight of the garden, and specifically, the tendency for locals to allow their animals to roam freely and munch on the precious plants. Amatis grew frustrated when Mr. Fitzwater's pigs repeatedly broke into the garden and devoured mulberry leaves. Despite his objections, the pigs came again and again, so Amatis took matters into his own hands and ordered the Trustee's servants to shoot the pigs on sight if they were spotted in the garden. Sure enough, the pigs came, and they ate. Sadly, the pig's owner complained of the shooting, and the servants met the same fate as many indentured servants in those early days. They were sentenced to a public whipping. Paul Amatis "took a disgust" and ran off to Charleston.

The person who would take over the silk industry was a woman who brought high hopes to the Georgia Trustees. Sadly, the woman (Mrs. Camuse) turned out to be one of the most troublesome, uncooperative, infuriating misbehavers of the entire colonial era.

19

TROUBLESOME WOMEN

T he early 1700s are not known as a time of women's empowerment. Most poor women of the era lived their lives as homemakers and child bearers, and their education was typically limited to the arts of cooking, caregiving, and gardening. However, every place and time in history can provide a few examples of women who pushed their boundaries and their luck to the limits of the law. Early Savannah was no different, and there were a few women who, upon finding a crack in the system, clutched their skirt hems and grabbed the powers to rule their own spheres and torment a few astonished men. One of the most surprised and dismayed was Mr. William Stephens.

Fair Hand and Foul Mouth

As far as English officials were concerned, the establish-ment of a successful silk industry was one of the most critical goals and obligations for Savannah. When the first Italian silk experts became frustrated and fled the town, the British government scrambled to find a replacement. As it turned out, they found one in the name of a certain Mrs. Camuse, another Italian with secret knowledge of the industry so desperately needed in the colony. At first, Mrs. Camuse seemed like a Godsend; she was admired for her leadership as, one by one, "proper girls" and "good Wives" turned up with "five, ten, twenty, even forty pounds worth of silk balls." The woman and her female army turned in 400 pounds of silk balls under Camuse's direction in the first year or so. But then things turned strange with Mrs. Camuse.

While Mrs. Camuse did oversee the successful production of silk balls, the woman kept the secrets of her trade to herself, much to the dismay of Mr. Stephens. The man did *attempt* to convince the woman to train a few young women in the handling of the worms and the delicate leaves, but she merely toyed with the frustrated official. When two young women from a nearby settlement were placed in the care of Mrs. Camuse as apprentices to the silk production business, they settled in to live with the woman for a full season. However, once their time with Camuse had come to an end, it became apparent that the girls were "Ignorant of what they went for," but they had been trained quite thoroughly in the art of housekeeping and serving!

William Stephens grew increasingly frustrated with the woman, claiming she was power hungry and egotistical, and Mrs. Camuse surely was a constant thorn in his side. She convinced Stephens to give her a house to expand her business, and then managed to have a few rooms added on for spinning the silk. She constantly demanded money and then claimed she hadn't been paid when, according to Stephens, she had been. Stephens was "startled" to find that Mrs. Camuse had schemed to travel to England with some silk balls and confront the Trustees, face to face. The relationship between Stephens and Camuse further deteriorated when Camuse demanded a gift of a horse and carriage, and

Stephens reminded her that he had provided those very items a year earlier, but they had sat idle at the town stable before being sold. Stephens complained in his journal that the woman was "a curious Artist," who fell into fits of "freaks." She was a bit too fond of the rum bottle, which often "set her agog." It soon became apparent that the fate of the settlement and the industry were partly in the hands of an unstable woman.

Mrs. Camuse continued to confound, frustrate, and torment Stephens, who could do little to control the situation. With each successful shipment of silk to London, the Trustees returned with expressions of praise. Stephens could hardly upset the one success of the colony by making an enemy of the one person who knew the industry secrets. In March of 1744, the poor man lamented in his journal that he was at his wit's end:

 The Mad frantick Behaviour of Mrs. Camuse, was more than Sufficient for one days Observations, who came and attacked me in my house, with such a parcell of Scurrilous words, and abusive Language, as I have Scarcely ever heard, which I was quite amazed at, not knowing wherein I had given her the least offence... The part she now acted was more like a Woman came out of Bedlam, than a rational Creature, raving, Clapping her hands, clinching her fist (which I expected every Minute she would bestow on me) and gave me no room (for a while that she toss'd to and fro) to offer a word ... After half an hour thus spent to give Vent to her passion, she threw her self out of doors, leaving me not one Jot more knowing what she meant, than when she began.[1]

It seems that the savvy Mrs. Camuse was a fluent speaker of French and Italian, so her rant had been delivered in a mix of languages that made little sense to poor Stephens. However, a week or so after this encounter, he did finally discover the reason for Mrs. Camuse's most recent outburst. She was infuriated to find that the house she'd been given had a loose board. Since the precious worms in her care were a favorite treat for rats and other vermin, the loose board may well have cost the village a year's worth of silk production.

The Cartographer's Wife

In the very same year that Mrs. Camuse descended upon the Stephens house, a dispute over a canoe erupted into turmoil and threatened the success of the colony. The defendant in this case was Mr. Joseph Avery, a skilled and important man in the town who had been appointed as the town surveyor. In his free time, Avery was a boat builder, providing many of the vessels used to travel to and from the several settlements and Charleston. But his official job was to determine boundary lines within the town perimeters, and to wander into the surrounding lands to explore and sketch out the swamps, streams, and rivers with his cartography skills.

The courtroom brouhaha started over a canoe that Avery had built for a client. At some point the deal went sour, and Mr. Avery was left with a debt as well as a verdict *against* him in the court of law. As a result, Avery began to behave "exceedingly ill" in the courtroom, cursing and "affronting the Magistrates at the Bench" despite being admonished several times for his actions. In fact, Avery left the courthouse and refused to return, so a warrant was executed on him at his home. When he refused to cooperate, he was locked up in the logg-house.

All of this made William Stephens extremely nervous. Avery's skills were valuable and rare, and the man was in the middle of sketching out a map of the lands surrounding Savannah. In those days, maps were like keys to a kingdom. They gave away all the secrets of a land, and were essential for the town's security and economy. Poor Mr. Stephens decided to visit Avery in jail, in an effort to smooth things out, but he found Avery "blustering and deaf to all perswasions." Avery preferred, instead, to sit in jail. After a week or so, the man grew tired of his confinement and agreed to return to court. The case was eventually settled, but Avery's feelings were not. Then Mr. Avery died.

If the courtroom drama made President Stephens nervous, the aftermath of Avery's death only increased his anxiety. Before the poor man's body was properly rested, Stephens paid a visit to Mrs. Avery, in an attempt to secure the map which was, as Stephens understood, nearly finished. But Mrs. Avery was no delicate flower, and Stephens found himself, once again, at the mercy of a stubborn woman. It was soon apparent that the Avery widow knew exactly what she had in her possession. When Stephens came knocking on her door, Mrs. Avery made it clear that the map that he was seeking was locked up in a secure location, and would stay in place until her own future was secure.

Stephens was surely dabbing his brow as he left the Widow Avery that first visit. His employers, the Georgia Trustees, had commissioned the map, and they were eagerly awaiting its delivery. Even parliament and the English monarchy must have had an interest in the map, since it was so critical to the survival of the colony—and, perhaps all of the colonies, since Savannah was the only barrier to Spanish Florida. Stephens had no one to turn to for assistance with the frustrating woman, however, since it would take six weeks or so for a message to arrive in London. He was forced to deal with Mrs. Avery on his own.

But it seemed that she was not acting alone. On November 3 of 1744, Stephens wrote in his journal that "The Widow Avery [was] persisting obstinately not to comply with what was demanded of her." He was certain that the woman had an advisor, someone who was bent on "making mischief in any Shape, to the Disturbance of the whole Colony." Stephens grew increasingly agitated about the situation, worried that the woman may sell the map to the colony's enemies—or even destroy the priceless object—out of spite. He sent a message demanding that she come to see him, but she "turned a deaf ear."

It was a month later when Mrs. Avery decided to soften her stance a bit and give Mr. Stephens a way out of his predicament. She agreed to allow the map to be kept in a lock box secured by two locks: she would have possession of one key and Mr. Stephens could take possession of the other, until a financial agreement could be met. In the end, a deal was struck, and Mrs. Avery was assured that she would be able to profit from the sales of the copies of the map, while the Georgia Trustees kept ownership of the original. Once the deal was settled, Mrs. Avery packed up her belongings and moved to Charleston, having secured a comfortable future for herself and her children.[2]

First Nations Princess

Even the briefest of visitors to Savannah will have heard the name of Mary Musgrove, who earned a place in the history books as interpreter for General Oglethorpe in the colony's early days. Few people realize, though, that Mary had a long, productive, notable, and somewhat controversial career in the colony, and was possibly the most industrious, influential and successful person in the town's early history. She knew her worth, and proved to be a powerful force in a world where men claimed all the legal advantages, and she even terrorized the occupants of the fledgling town at one point, just to make a point.

Mary was married several times, so she operated under three different names in and around Savannah environs. She co-operated a trading post as Mary Matthews, and became extremely respected and influential among the Creeks. This position led to a longstanding battle with English authorities when it came to land ownership. Being a noble member of our First Nations, she was granted native lands on several occasions. The English did not necessarily respect the authority of the Native Americans to make such decisions, however, so Mary was repeatedly denied rights and owner- ship of lands she had been granted. At one point, she became fed up.

It was a quiet evening around 5 o'clock p.m., when the beat of the drum sounded through the streets, calling out an alarm. It appeared that a large number of First Nations men were streaming into town, and Mary was leading the way. A rumor spread quickly that Colonel Stephens' head had been cut off. The entire town gathered in one square in a panic, everyone wielding their arms. Luckily, Colonel Stephens showed up and, in an attempt to sooth everyone's nerves, announced to the crowd that he was not headless, and that the Indians were unarmed and peaceful. Meanwhile, a few of the town officials had secretly managed to separate Mary from her would-be warriors, and carried her quietly to jail. As the officials had suspected, this invasion was an attempt by Mary to shake up the town and demand a little respect.

Having recently lost another court battle for land that she claimed, she had designed to make a statement. She had accumulated this posse of supporters from the First Nations and successfully astonished Savannah hoping to push forward her claim to three of the coastal islands. Her plan backfired a little, as the officials managed to engineer a bit of trickery when they carried her off to jail. During that separation, they plied the natives with food and rum and sent them on their way.

Mary was not one to give up. While she lost this particular battle, she persisted in her claims to the Sea Islands, and was finally partly successful. In 1760, the British government granted her full title to St. Catherine's Island. She lived there until she died, and is buried there today.[3]

20

SWAMP THINGS

As reality set in among Savannah settlers that their destiny was to shield the more valuable South Carolina colony, the threats that lurked in the surrounding, steamy swamps grew increasingly threatening. It's no surprise that the colony grew more fearful of the alligators as time passed. It's likely that the beasts grew to enormous lengths in those days, and in great numbers, since they would have had few enemies before the town was settled. The town's fears were addressed once and for all, by Oglethorpe, who had one of the beasts captured and tied up, so the boys of the town could beat it to death to the cheers of a crowd.[1]

The ordeal may have helped for a short time, but there were frequent tales of other beasts lurking in the surrounding swamps. Stories spread of wild tigers roaming around in the woods, William Stephens complained that his plantation had been overrun by bears, which were having their way with his pigs.[2]

And there was an even greater concern. Among the distractions was the constant worry that their territory would be encroached upon—or even attacked—by the dastardly Florida Spaniards, who claimed this territory long before the settlers arrived. These fears were well founded, for there were several scuffles and battles over the years, but one early account sheds light on the fear that lingered. The Spanish could show up any time, it was feared, and in any place.

Spanish Spies

One April afternoon in 1738, a servant of Bailiff Henry Parker was working on a farm outside of town, when four strange men suddenly appeared before him. As they drew closer, one of them raised a sword and, in broken English, made it very clear that he was about to cut the man's throat.

Fortunately, another of the strangers calmed the other, and managed to convey that the servant's life would be spared if he would follow their instruction. It seemed that the men were looking for a place to rest and find a little refreshment, so they entered the farmhouse and told the man to stand guard at the door and warn them if he saw anyone else approaching.

The servant did as he was instructed, and stood lookout in the doorway while the men ransacked the house for a few hours and ate what food they could find. Finally, the men signaled that they were ready to leave. They forced the man to swear that he would not report the incident, before they set off into the woods, giving every impression that they were fully familiar with the local paths and trails. In reporting the event later, the man said that the mysterious, Spanish speaking intruders had long, dark hair worn in braids that were tucked up into their hats. They were dressed alike, in dark-colored clothing, and they used straps to tie their shoes instead of buckles. They were each armed with swords, guns, and pistols.[3]

Fugitives on the Run

Another peril of traveling in the piney woods and muddy marshes around Savannah was the possibility of running into those dastardly characters who used the woods to secret themselves away for one reason or another. Spanish spies were always a threat, but fugitives from Charleston also found the tidal streams around Savannah to be an appealing place to hide out. One day the town was abuzz with news that two fugitives had escaped from the Charleston jail and were suspected of having slaughtered some of the cattle grazing in the cow pens on the Savannah, just north of Hutchinson Island. As a safety measure, Oglethorpe ordered that two men be stationed on the bank of the Savannah with a promise of a ten pound reward for the capture of the absconders. They were given a swivel gun and instructed to watch for a suspicious looking canoe. It was morning when they spied "something looking like a canoe," and supposed the structure to be the escaped prisoners. They informed Oglethorpe, and the general gathered two brave men to assist in a scheme to entrap the men. They hid away in a bend, quietly waiting for the canoe to approach. As it grew closer, it soon became apparent that they were stalking a large tree floating in the river.

While this was a disappointing turn of events, the following days proved more encouraging. The fugitives were discovered by a few Yamacraw scouts and turned over to Oglethorpe. They were put on a small boat and escorted to Beaufort, where they were turned over to Charleston officials.[4]

Lost in the Swamp

The swamps surrounding the Savannah settlement were

dark, perilous, and difficult to navigate, as one incident from early days will demonstrate.

In today's terms, the southside of Savannah seems like a mere stone's throw from the main town. However, in the eighteenth century, a journey to this remote end of town could be deadly, and even the most skilled woodsman could have serious trouble navigating the rugged terrain.

At some point during his stay in Savannah, Reverend George Whitfield decided to journey southward to visit the fortification of Frederica, which was a daunting eighty miles away from town. To reach the fort by water, it was first necessary to travel by horseback to Vernon River Landing, a place that was, in itself, a few miles south of Savannah. It was customary for friends to accompany a traveler on the first leg of his journey, and Whitfield was joined by a young man named Habersham. Young Mr. Habersham would ride along to Vernon Landing and return to Savannah with both horses.

Once the men reached the launching place, Habersham made an ill-fated decision concerning his trip back to Savannah. He was now traveling alone, and he decided to attempt to cut a shorter path through the swamp. It wasn't long before he regretted this decision, as his beloved horse soon became mired in the swamp, and with each attempt to free the beast, the horse only sunk lower in the muck. Habersham soon realized he would have to abandon his horse for the time being and make the homeward journey on the other horse. He tied the stuck horse to a tree and trekked along through the night with much difficulty, and, "after much Wandering and Fatigue," arrived back home in the morning. The next day, he gathered a few friends to help him retrieve his horse from the swamps.

The men rode into the dark swamp together, but soon found the landscape was so challenging that they became separated. Before long, they were each wandering aimlessly, unable to find one another *or* the horse they'd set off to rescue. After much time and plenty of hardship, the two friends finally found their way back to Savannah, but Habersham did not. This time, officials sent out search parties who were to remain in pairs and fire shots in the air to mark their locations. To help with their search, officials also hired a few skilled native trackers. Nonetheless, the hunt for the missing lad went on, unsuccessfully, for days.

On the shores of the Vernon River was a small German settlement called Hampstead. It was a quaint little settlement, described by an early traveler to be a "pretty" agricultural town where the inhabitants lived in huts and grew produce that they would sell in the Savannah market. One member of this settlement had heard of the missing lad, and he was so moved by the situation that he set off on his own. Amazingly, it was a short time later that he fired his piece and heard a faint response. It was poor Mr. Habersham, who had been wandering for three days and nights with no food or clean water.

Mr. Habersham was overjoyed to see his rescuer, and stated that he had just "laid down, expecting never to have risen again" when he heard the searcher's gun. The man carried Habersham back to his hut, gave him milk and a little food before he "brought him joyfully to Town."[5]

John Wesley's Daring Escape

Whitfield was not the only Savannah minister traipsing the woods, as it turns out. John Wesley, Savannah's famous evangelist and co-founder of the Methodist movement, had to make a hasty retreat from the town after a little trouble over a woman. (That story comes a bit later on.) The tale of his experience in the southern swamps is harrowing and representative of the trouble that Savannah's environs presented in the early days before roads and bridges improved the journey.

The plan was for the men to travel by land to Charleston, where Wesley could catch a ship to London. The problem was that land travel was treacherous under the best of conditions, and there were only a few guides who knew the route. Wesley had left in the dark without a real guide; instead, he was accompanied by a few loyal followers from town who wanted to make sure that the clergyman made it safely to his destination. The small boat made its way up the Savannah River to a small town, where the men set off on foot. It wasn't long before they were lost.

Luckily, they did run into a farmer in the woods, who showed them a path that was marked by tree blazings, or notches cut from the tree barks. They followed the trail for a time, but realized that they had wandered off the path, as they could find no trees with the telltale notches. Furthermore, they had no food but a small gingerbread cake that they split between them.

The men carried on through the night, wading through swamp that was chest high at times. The next day, they found themselves running into the same farmer again, realizing they'd traveled in a circle. The farmer set them on another path, and they continued on, but struggled from thirst, as they had no fresh water.

Now growing desperate, the men began digging into the soil with bare hands. Miraculously, they found fresh water after clawing a few feet into the ground. After stumbling and nearly perishing for several days, they came upon a plantation in South Carolina, where they found shelter and help for the rest of their journey. Eventually, Wesley did make it to Charleston, were he managed to secure passage to England.[6]

The Beasts of Hutchinson Island

It was always a struggle, trying to find a way to keep hundreds of heads of cattle close enough to the town that they could be accessible for butchering as needed. Much of the cattle were allowed to roam free, so they would not deplete the edible grass in a single location. Smaller groups of cattle would be kept in a confined space, and men would refresh the confined groups occasionally, by going out into the swamps to round up a few at a time. This process was complicated by the fact that predators lurked in the woods, both human and beast.

The first idea for keeping cattle close at hand seemed logical enough. When the town was first settled, it was determined that the most convenient place to manage the livestock in this way was to place them across the Savannah River, on Hutchinson Island. There would be natural barriers in the way of rivers that surrounded the island, so the cattle could graze freely, but they couldn't wander off too far and get lost in the swamps. However, that idea did not pan out as expected:

 Soon after the first Setting down of the Colony, 'twas order'd that half a Dozen Cows and a Bull should be put on Hutchinsons Island, which was just opposite to this Town, to take their Chance, whether to live or die, the whole Island being Swamp Land, and great part of it overflow'd at some Seasons; besides that it was in an extraordinary manner infested with Bears and Alligators... the first Original Stock of half a Dozen ... increased to near 20 ... [then] fell back again to their first number, Sometimes perishing by Wild Beasts.[7]

Local Travel

Savannah was somewhat isolated in the early days, and the lack of roads and bridges inland from the town made managing one's country property dangerous and difficult:

 The want of roads is grievously complained of by almost every man here. Several people are obliged to go to their Lotts thro' Swamps up to the middle in water: which not only prevents their bringing any Crop home; but is the Cause that men get Violent Illness in Winter Time by being wet and cold as they pass through those deep Swamps.[8]

Travel by water was much faster than travel by land. A journey to Charleston would take several days by sea, since it was sometimes necessary to wait for friendly tides, waves, and winds, although it was common to travel in a long boat with six rowers. By land, the journey took even longer. A traveler would have to start by going up river several miles by canoe or a long vessel called a periagua, and then set off on foot for a difficult hike through swamps and woods.

In June of 1743, William Stephens set off on a trip over land to survey some northern lands. He took a canoe with rowers fourteen miles upriver to a good landing spot. When they set off on foot, the job of the rowers was to clear the path as they hiked. At night, he slept on a buffalo hide on the ground. They made fires near them as they slept to "keep off vermin." During the journey, one of the men in the party fell ill, but there was no one amongst them who was familiar with the art of bloodletting, so the man was spared that treatment.[9]

21

HEARTSTRINGS

Modern Savannah is known for honeymoons and hauntings, so it is only fitting to conclude with a look at love and death in the early settlement. It is clear that passions ran high in the little colony, wedged precariously between a vast ocean and a never-ending stretch of swampy wilds.

Death and Robbery

Mr. Jacob Matthews was the second husband of Mary Musgrove, and the two spent much of their lives toiling at their trading post a short way up the Savannah River from the main town. They ran a successful enterprise together, and the two enjoyed a fine house in Savannah, as well as their dwelling at the trading post location. In 1742, Mr. Matthews fell deathly ill, and Mrs. Matthews moved her household to their country home, where she and her servants could care for the man.

A shocking turn of events commenced shortly after. While the town home was vacated, some evildoer plotted to rob poor Mr. Matthews of all his valuable possessions. The robber absconded with all the most valuable household goods, as well as "2 or 3 suits of wearing apparel, trimmed with gold and silver lace" and a valuable watch.

Before long, some of the valuables were found in the possession of "a woman among the Dutch servants." It seemed she was attempting to sell the goods, but she insisted that she was not the one who had stolen the items. Instead, she pointed the finger at an outcast among the native people, formerly of Yamacraw, who had known the Matthews couple from his dealings at the trading post.

Word around town suggested that the woman in possession of the goods was an idle sort, but she had lately married a tinker in town, and the man was a respected member of the community who had no idea of his wife's clandestine activities. Gossip of the ordeal spread quickly through the Savannah streets, and before the authorities could catch up with the woman, a bundle appeared at the doorstep of the Matthews home. Sure enough, when authorities opened the bundle, they found all of the stolen goods inside.

Savannah authorities decided not to press charges against the woman, but the Yamacraw natives were not so forgiving. They dispatched a band to hunt down the thief, with orders to shoot him on sight. Luckily for the thief, there is no indication that they ever caught up with him.

Mr. Matthews did succumb to his illness in the day or so after the robbery. His funeral was large, with most of the town in attendance. He was given a military send-off, with "8 minute guns to be fired at his internment."[1]

An Elegant Funeral

Many of the men who died in Savannah received some level of military honors at their burials, since Savannah was a defensive outpost and every able-bodied man was required to serve in the militia. But one of the best surviving descriptions of an early Savannah funeral was that of a woman who came to the settlement along with George Whitfield. She worked with the famous clergyman as he established the orphanage outside of town, and she apparently cared for many of the children living there.

The woman died in March of 1740 and was buried the next day in a solemn affair. Her body was accompanied on its way to the church by "thirty or forty little boys and girls" who marched in pairs singing Psalms as they went. The children led the way, and Mr. Whitfield followed. After them, "half a dozen distinguished men" walked "holding up the pall." As the procession marched along, it was joined on the route by other townspeople. Another group of people were waiting at the church when the procession arrived. Mr. Whitfield performed the ceremony, and afterward, "the corpse was carried to the common place of burial, and there interred in the usual manner."

A Scalawag Burial

Mr. William Aglionby would have won no popularity contest in Colonial Savannah. He was a "pretended lawyer," who ran an illegal pub in Savannah, where he frustrated William Stephens immensely for selling rum without a license. He died in the morning of August 28, 1738, and was buried, unceremoniously, the very same evening.

According to Mr. Stephens, it was better to bury the man without any attempt at fanfare, since "His character was better forgot, than remembered to his infamy." Although he was said to have come from a respectable family and "had the appearance of some education," Aglionby was a notorious "stirrer up of ill Blood." It should come as no surprise, that this town, which amused itself by throwing strangers in stocks and dangling milk maidens from the sides of a ship, had little empathy for a man who had the reputation of being a snake in the courtroom and a troublemaker in the town.

Stephens claimed the man died from overconsumption of rum, and that the death was no great loss to the colony. During the man's sickness, there were visits and attempts to pray for his soul, but those offers were rebuffed. His funeral service was read by a servant, as Mr. Whitfield (minister at the time), "very justly" refused to serve that office. Instead, Whitfield went to the place where the body was interred and made a speech, a "pathetick Exhortation to the people," to be steadfast to the principles of Christianity. He warned the pitiful group of would-be mourners to be mindful in their endeavors, and to avoid being "seduced into damnable errors" in their lives.

After the abrupt and inelegant service, poor Mr. Aglionby was finally left to find peace in the colonial cemetery.[2]

Mad Love

A curious thing happened at a cow pen located outside of town, when a group of servants was offered a bundle of English "biskets" that were sent by boat from Savannah as a sweet treat for the men. One man, when handed the treat, "cursed and swore" and "threw away with hands and feet the Bisket." He then "threatened a man with his Fist to beat him seasonably." The crazed man continued to throw a fit and ran off wildly, jumping like a madman upon the doctor's fence trying to tear it down.

At some point, this man ran into the woods with a companion servant and found a group of people working there, most likely sawing timber. He told the people that they should go to their minister and call him a "Black Devil," and tell him he should go to hell.

While the townsfolk were shocked and mystified by the man's strange behavior, the local minister was not. The minister had recently paid the man a visit and insisted that he stop visiting the home of a certain young woman in town. This girl was the daughter of a widow who was frequently away from home.

Despite the minister's warning, the man had paid a clandestine nighttime visit to the young girl, while the mother was away. The two were discovered by one of the town's inhabitants "under the house roof, in a very scandalous posture."

At the end of his rope, the minister paid a visit to the Savannah magistrates, who wrote up a warrant for the servant's arrest. He was taken in, and ordered to pay a healthy sum as bond, in the promise that he would behave and not see the girl again. It seems that the man was driven to misbehave by the torment of forbidden love.[3]

Unrequited Love

John Wesley is most noted for being the founder of the Methodist movement, and this icon spent several months in the little Georgia settlement, leading a flock of devoted followers, before he had to make a hasty, secretive departure in the dark of the night. His abrupt retreat came about, for the most part, to avoid spending some time in the Savannah jail. As in most scandals, this man's problems started with a woman. His is, perhaps, the most famous love story to emerge from Savannah's early days. Alas, it is not one with a happy ending.

Wesley arrived in Savannah in 1736, and it wasn't long before a lovely young woman named Sophy Hopkey caught his eye. Sophy was the niece of Thomas Causton, the very same, powerful Mr. Causton, who served as chief judge and storekeeper. The young woman had once been attached to a Mr. Mellichamp in Savannah, but, sadly, he was the same Mr. Mellichamp who was convicted of counterfeiting and was, by the time Wesley came onto the scene, spending time in a Charleston jail. It might be important to note that Mellichamp carried a flame for Sophy, and had (from his jail cell) threatened to kill Sophy and anybody she might marry.

It might have been that, or it might have been his religious devotion that prevented John Wesley from asking Sophy to be his wife, for it wasn't long before he'd become totally besotted with the eighteen year old lass. There is some indication that she returned the feelings, but she did become impatient when it became increasingly clear that the clergyman had no intention of marrying her. Everyone was surprised when she suddenly married a newcomer to town, a Mr. William Williamson. Nobody was more surprised than John Wesley. Records show that the man was heartbroken.

Because Savannah was such as small town in the wilderness, it was inevitable that Sophy and Wesley would cross paths. She avoided his sermons and services for weeks, but she did decide to return to church in August of 1737. When she did, she received a monumental snub that humiliated her and infuriated her husband and her powerful uncle. When Sophy came forth for the reception of the Sacrament, Wesley refused her and would not allow her access to the bread and wine of Holy Communion. The snub, and Sophy's humiliation, were the talk of the church, and soon the entire town.

Thomas Causton was incensed. Sophy's husband was infuriated. Both men vowed revenge on the minister, and it wasn't long before Causton convinced a grand jury under his control to return a bill of indictment against Wesley, for several charges indicating deviant behavior. Wesley was instructed to remain on call for an impending court date.

Weeks passed, and Wesley, being no fool, realized that his future in Savannah was doomed. He posted a notice at the courthouse, declaring his intent to leave town to return to London. When Causton heard of this, he declared it unlawful, and instructed all the lawmen of Savannah to be on the lookout for Wesley trying to leave. Nonetheless, Wesley did manage to leave, in the dark of night, in a small rowing craft, with three men to accompany him.

The story is not completely somber, for there is every indication that Sophy and William lived a happy life together after Wesley fled. There is no indication that Mr. Mellichamp murdered either of them when he was freed from jail. In fact, a visit to the Colonial Park Cemetery in Savannah reveals that the oldest identifiable grave belongs to a Mr. William Williamson.

A Simple Explanation

Samuel Pensyre had a good life in Savannah. He'd arrived with his loving wife in August of 1733 and initially settled on Tybee Island, but soon had to relocate to Savannah because his land became a salt marsh at every spring tide, which made it impossible to grow crops. He was a well-respected doctor, who saved many patients with his knowledge of healing plants; however, he did seem to struggle against the tyranny of Thomas Causton, who refused to pay him for his healing work.

Pensyre seemed happy in Savannah, until the day a letter arrived in the mail from Mr. Oglethorpe. He must have opened the letter with apprehension, as there could be few reasons that the general would pen a personal note.

But then, Pensyre *surely* suspected the reason for the

letter. As he read it, his concern was justified, and it was clear that Mr. Pensyre had some explaining to do. Oglethorpe had written to ask why the man now lived happily in Savannah with his wife, when he had left another wife back in England.

What a dreadful task it must have been to take pen in hand and explain the circumstances that had led to his current situation.

"Honorable Sir," the letter began. "I lived happily with my wife in England for seven years, but ten years in total." The rest of his words (paraphrased and edited for clarity) tell a story of both misery and hope:

Toward the end of our time together, she got acquainted with some people that was debauched in their drinking that cursed liquor that was called Geneva [gin]. When she got in that way of drinking, she could not leave it off, and generally got drunk almost every day. Everything I tried in attempt to hinder her was in vain. At last, my life began to be very troublesome to me, and I was ashamed of her, both for drinking and swearing and cursing, so that I could not bear it any longer.

I thought in myself that I should not offend God as much, as if I remained with her and be forever quarreling with her about her abominable way of drunkness, which is well known about London. I had nothing but strife, and I was incapable of getting my bread or serving God. Eventually, she tried to destroy herself by drinking liquid laudanum, and if I had not taken a great deal of care to give her a vomit, she would have been a dead woman.

As such, I was forced to go away from her. After a while, I met with this woman now in Georgia with me. She carried herself as sober and chaste as any woman ever did, or ever will do. We concluded both to go to Georgia. But, if your honor would have my old wife come to me, I would receive her, though not willingly. I know very well that she will never keep herself from drinking, and when she is drinking, so is also mad.[4]

While his letter seemed contrite enough, the unfortunate but cunning Mr. Pensyre concluded his letter with an observation clearly designed to make Mr. Oglethorpe think twice. Pensyre was the only man of medicine in town at the time, and the town was in desperate need for medical care. The death rate was rising, and the colony had already lost the first doctor who'd arrived on the *Ship Anne*. "I am sensible that I would not be able to continue what I've been obliged to do," he wrote. "I hope your honor will take this into consideration."

It is not entirely clear whether the old Mrs. Pensyre traveled to Savannah to be with her lawful husband, but it is doubtful. The journey, alone, after all of the preparations, would have taken six months. There is no record of her arriving in Savannah. In fact, the only other record of Samuel Pensyre appears a few years later, when he, himself, succumbed to the harsh life in Savannah. He died in 1735 and we are left to hope that he left this world with a sober, loving wife by his side.

Weddings En Masse

There seemed to be an urgency to populate the town in its early days, and to see young people married off early and often. Fortunately, young people seemed eager enough to be married. There were several settlements springing up beyond the limits of Savannah proper, and in those outposts, ministers could be hard to come by. For this reasons, there were a few occasions when groups of couples would travel to Savannah to be married, all in one gigantic ceremony.

In 1732, six couples arrived in Savannah from the nearby

settlement of Purysburgh, South Carolina. The urgency of this crowd was clear: it was noted that "some of these wives will hardly stay the nine months out to create a progeny," There was a suggestion of premarital hanky-panky with the claim that a child might appear "either by reason of the fruit-fulness of the air or by Tryal of the skill beforehand."

Mr. Oglethorpe agreed to perform the ceremony, and he marked the happy occasion by ordering a fine hog to be killed for the entertainment of the company. Beer, wine, and punch flowed, and everyone in attendance was very merry and "danced the whole night long" to the music of a fiddle. The couples and their families stayed the night in Savannah before boarding a boat to return up the Savannah River to their town. As they embarked, the craft was saluted with a few shots from a large canon.[5]

Mary's Grand Wedding

At some point while Mary Musgrove-Matthews was nursing her poor, ailing husband on his deathbed, she apparently caught the eye of the current Savannah minister, Mr. Thomas Bosomworth. It is not that surprising, as Mary was surely a fascinating figure. For a start, she was, at one point, the wealthiest landowner in Georgia. She was worldly, having served the colony as interpreter and having traveled to London to meet King George II in 1734. She was a fighter, having fended off a physical attack by the lunatic Joseph Watson, and having fended off the English government for her land rights. It would seem that Mary was easy to love.

The town was shocked by the announcement of the marriage between Mary and Minister Bosomworth. It was a happy union for both, as the minister was undoubtedly smitten, and Mary had found herself in a higher social ranking than ever before. English clergy enjoyed a respectable level of social status in Georgian times, and this must have been attractive to Mary.

Although they married privately, the couple thought it proper to share their happy news with the entire town. There was a grand celebration, held in the biggest trustee-owned house in the town, one that was occupied by President William Stephens at the time. Stephens cleared several rooms of his home, and workmen assembled several long tables, each capable of seating twenty guests. The tables were filled with an assortment of cold meats, and glasses were filled with wine and punch.

After dinner, the entertainment began, as a fiddler played and merry couples swung arm in arm, in groups of eight or ten couples at a time. The celebration lasted for hours, and the dancers stayed well into the night as the festive music floated through the streets of Savannah. Mary Musgrove-Matthews-Bosomworth was, arguably, the most intriguing character to grace Colonial Savannah. She was born an First Nations princess, and, on that night of celebration, she must have felt like the queen of the entire Georgia colony.[6]

NOTES

1. Head Smacks And Horse Parades

1. E. Merton Coulter and Albert Berry Saye, *A List of the Early Settlers of Georgia* (Baltimore, Genealogical Pub Co.,1983): http://dlg.galileo.usg.edu/ugapressbks/do-pdf:ugp9780820334394. This full book is published online.

2. Edward J. Cashin, ed, *Setting Out to Begin a New World: Colonial Georgia: A Documentary History*, (Savannah, GA: Beehive Press, 1995), 16; Robert G. McPherson, ed., "The Voyage of the Anne--a Daily Record," *Georgia Historical Quarterly* 44, no. 2 (June 1960): 226, https://www.jstor.org/stable/40578050?seq=1.

3. Peter Gordon, "An Account of the First Settling of the Colony of Georgia with a Journal of the First Embarkation, Under the Direction of Mr. Oglethorpe," [1730/1750], in *Southeastern Native American Documents, 1730-1842, Georgia Historical Collections* (Savannah), 30-31, https://dlg.usg.edu/record/dlg_zlna_krc089#item.

4. Gordon, *Colony of Georgia*, 30-31; McPherson, "The Voyage of the Anne," 227.

5. McPherson, "The Voyage of the Anne."

6. Gordon, Colony of Georgia, 32.

7. Francis Moore, "A Voyage to Georgia," in *Georgia Historical Collections* (Savannah, Georgia, 1840), 12.

8. From Viscount Percival, *Diary of the Earl of Egmont* (London: Royal Commission on Historical Manuscripts), vol. II, 408.

9. Kenneth Coleman and Sarah B. Gober Temple, *Georgia Journeys: Being an Account of the Lives of Georgia's Original Settlers and Many Other Early Settlers* (Athens: University of Georgia Press, 2010), 77.

2. The Peacekeepers

1. *Colonial Records of the State of Georgia*, eds. Kenneth Coleman and Milton Ready, vol. 20, *Original Papers, Correspondence to the Trustees, James Oglethorpe, and Others, 1732-1735* (Athens: University of Georgia Press, 1982), 194. Tythingmen were paid five pounds each per year and constables were paid ten pounds per year. *Colonial Records*, ed. Allen D. Candler, vol. 2, *1732-1752* (Athens: University of Georgia Press, 1904), 417.

2. *Colonial Records*, ed. Allen D. Candler, vol. 4, *Stephens's Journal, 1737-1740* (Atlanta: Franklin Printing and Publishing, 1906), *147*. Note the spelling of "jail," which was sometimes gaol and sometimes goal.

3. *Colonial Records*, 4, 168.

4. Trustees for Establishing the Colony of Georgia in America, "Letters from Georgia, vol. 14200, 1732-1735 June," in *Transcripts of the Earl of Egmont Papers*, *Georgia Historical Collections* (Savannah, Georgia), 325, http://dig.galileo.usg.edu/do:guan_ms1786_ms1786-14200; *Colonial Records*, vol. 20, 336.

5. *Colonial Records*, ed. Lucian Lamar Knight, vol. 24, *Original Papers: Correspondence, Trustees, General Oglethorpe and Others, 1735-1752* (Atlanta: Chas. P. Byrd, 1915), 171.

6. A list of lots awarded to colonists can be found in William Harden, *History of Savannah and South Georgia* (New York: Lewis Publishing Company, 1913).

7. *Colonial Records*, ed. Lucian Lamar Knight, vol. 22, pt. 2, *Original Papers: Correspondence, Trustees, General Oglethorpe and Others, 1735-1752* (Atlanta: Chas. P. Byrd Press, 1913), 85.

8. *Colonial Records*, vol. 22, pt. 1, 237-239.

9. William Stephens, *A Journal of the Proceedings in Georgia* (1742; repr., Ann Arbor: Chamblin Bookmine, 1966), 292-293.

3. Disorder In The Courts

1. *Colonial Records*, vol. 4, 259, 313.

2. *Colonial Records*, vol. 4, 260.

3. *Colonial Records*, vol. 4, 27, 63, 83, 146.

4. *Colonial Records*, vol. 4, 170-175.

4. Torture Devices

1. Patrick Telfer et al., *A True and Historical Narrative of the Colony of Georgia, in America: From the First Settlement Thereof Until This Present Period; Containing the Most Authentick Facts, Maters, and Transactions Therein; Together with His Majesty's Charter, Representations of the People, Letters, Etc, and a Dedication to His Excellency General Oglethorpe* (Charleston: Printed by Timothy, for the authors, 1741; repr., Washington: P. Force, 1835), 26.

2. Alice Morse Earle, *Curious Punishments of Bygone Days* (Chicago: Herbert S. Stone & Co., 1896), 71; *Colonial Records*, ed. Allen D. Candler, vol. 19, *Statutes, Colonial and Revolutionary, 1768-1805* (Atlanta: Chas. P. Byrd Press, 1911), 346.

3. *Colonial Records*, vol. 19, 159.

4. "Letters from Georgia, vol. 14200," 157; Coleman and Temple, *Georgia Journeys*, 120; Earle, *Curious Punishments*, 26.

5. "Letters from Georgia, vol. 14200," 157; *Colonial Records*, vol. 21, *Original Papers; Correspondence, Trustees, General Oglethorpe, and Others, 1735-1752* (Atlanta: Charles P. Byrd, 1923), 249.

6. *Colonial Records*, ed. Allen D. Candler, vol. 6, *Proceedings of the President and Assistants from October 12, 1741-October 30, 1754* (Atlanta: Franklin Printing and Publishing, 1906), 106-164.

7. Harden, *History of Savannah*, 22.

8. *Colonial Records*, vol. 20, 373, vol. 22, 253.

9. *Colonial Records*, ed. Allen D. Candler, vol. 18, *Statutes Enacted by the Royal Legislature of Georgia from Its First Session in 1754-1768* (Atlanta: Chas P. Byrd, 1910), 787.

5. Pickpockets And Prostitutes

1. *Colonial Records*, vol. 4, 464–465; Currency converted to modern equivalent with Eric W. Nye, *Pounds Sterling to Dollars: Historical Conversion of Currency*, accessed February 20, 2021, https://www.uwyo.edu/numimage/currency.htm.

2. "Advertisement," *Georgia Gazette*, August 17, 1768 (2,2).

3. *Letters to Georgia*, vol. 14200, 44.

4. *Colonial Records*, vol. 21, 57.

5. Gordon, *Colony of Georgia*, 40–42.

6. *Colonial Records*, vol. 20, 456.

6. Colonial Crimes

1. *Colonial Records*, vol. 21, 288.

2. William Kilty, *British Statutes in Force in Maryland According to the Report Made to the General Assembly*, vol. I (Baltimore: M. Curlander, 1912), 211.

3. *Colonial Records*, vol. 4, 166–171, 646.

4. *Colonial Records*, vol. 4, 138, 451–455; *New England Weekly Journal* (Boston), September 21, 1736, 2.

5. *Colonial Records*, vol. 4, 94.

6. *Georgia Gazette* (Savannah, GA), February 21, 1765, 2.

7. *The New York Gazette* (New York), September 3, 1767, 3.

8. *Colonial Records*, vol. 4, 639–40.

7. Murder And Evidence

1. *Colonial Records*, vol. 4 supplement, 8–12, 23–27.
2. *Colonial Records*, vol. 4 supplement,125–182.
3. Stephens, *A Journal of the Proceedings*, 381; Colonial Records, vol. 4, 366–368, 382.
4. E. Merton Coulter, *Journal of William Stephens*, vol. II (Athens: University of Georgia Press, 1959), 53, 67–68.

8. Everyday Life And Public Places

1. *Colonial Records*, vol. 20, 17, 392.
2. *Colonial Records*, vol. 20, 17.
3. "Letters from Georgia, vol. 14200," 24.
4. Trustees for Establishing the Colony of Georgia in America, "Letters from Georgia, vol. 14203, 1737 June-1739 January," in *Transcripts of the Earl of Egmont papers, Georgia Historical Collections* (Savannah, GA), 136–164, https://dlg.usg.edu/record/guan_ms1786_ms1786-14203.
5. *Colonial Records*, vol. 20, 85.
6. *Colonial Records*, vol. 20, 159–60.
7. *Colonial Records*, vol. 20, 357; *Colonial Records*, ed. Allen D. Candler, vol. 5, *Journal of the Earl of Egmont, first president of the Board of Trustees from June 14, 1738 to May 25, 1744* (Atlanta: Franklin Printing and Publishing, 1904), 605.
8. *Colonial Records*, vol. 20, 394.
9. *Colonial Records*, ed. Lucian Lamar Knight, vol. 26, *Original Papers: Trustees, President and Assistants and Others, 1750-1752* (Atlanta: Chas. P. Byrd, 1916), 59.
10. *Colonial Records*, vol. 4, 377.
11. *Colonial Records*, vol. 4 supplement, 27.
12. Colonial Records, vol. 19, 19; "Household Bread," OED online, Oxford University Press, accessed March 2021, http://oed/view/entry88908?redirectedFrom=household+bread#eid1357635
13. "Letters from Georgia, vol. 14203," 148.
14. *Georgia Gazette* (Savannah, GA), July 29, 1767, 3.

9. The Drinking Time

1. *Colonial Records*, vol. 4, 122; vol. 20, 17, 368; Cashin, *Setting Out*, 29; Coleman and Temple, *Georgia Journeys*, 25.
2. *Colonial Records*, vol. 20, 239.
3. Gordon, *Colony of Georgia*, 45–46.
4. Gordon, 36.

5. Coulter, *Journal of William Stephens*, vol. II, 150.

10. Troublesome Servants

1. "Letters from Georgia, vol. 14203," 232.
2. Noelle Gallagher, *Itch, Clap, Pox: Venereal Disease in the Eighteenth-century Imagination* (United Kingdom: Yale University Press, 2018), 134; *Colonial Records*, vol. 21, 45.
3. *Colonial Records*, vol. 4, 86; vol. 20, 466.
4. *Colonial Records*, vol. 22, pt. 2, 496.
5. *Colonial Records*, vol. 22, pt. 2, 174–175.
6. *Colonial Records*, vol. 20, 87; "Letters from Georgia, vol. 14200," 113.
7. *Colonial Records*, vol. 20, 241–259.

11. Fisticuffs And Musket Shots

1. *Colonial Records*, vol. 4 supplement, 207–210.
2. *Colonial Records*, vol. 4, 648.
3. "Letters from Georgia, vol. 14203," 3–5.
4. "Letters from Georgia, vol. 14203," 5–6.

12. Scoops, Gossip, And Scandals

1. *Georgia Gazette* (Savannah, GA), January 13, 1768, 4; September 8, 1763, 3.
2. *Colonial Records*, vol. 20, 391.
3. *Colonial Records*, vol. 22, 241; vol. 5, 80.
4. *Colonial Records*, vol. 21, pt. 1, 203.
5. *Colonial Records*, vol. 5, 140; Proceedings, 255.
6. *Colonial Records*, vol. 4 supplement, 95, 97, 104, 107, 170–176; Proceedings, 431.

13. Pirates, Shipwrecks, And Scallawags

1. *Colonial Records*, vol. 18, 25.
2. "Escape from Prison." *Alexandria Gazette & Daily Advertiser* (Alexandria, VA), June 4, 1819: [3]. *Readex: America's Historical Newspapers*
3. *New England Weekly Journal* (Boston), August 27, 1733, 1. *Readex: America's Historical Newspapers*.
4. *Colonial Records*, vol. 4 supplement, 97, 225–227.
5. *Colonial Records*, vol. 4 supplement, 240.

6. "Extract of a Letter from Capt. Lancelot Davison of the Ship Lousia," *Alexandria Advertiser and Commercial Intelligencer* (Alexandria), Savannah, March 20, 1801.

14. First Nations Problems

1. "Extract of a Letter from the Recorder of Savannah," *The Boston Weekly News-Letter* (Boston), October 24, 1734.
2. Mary Musgrove is widely known for serving as an interpreter for Oglethorpe in the early days, but the woman was much more fascinating than that one episode of her life, as this episode demonstrates. While she's addressed as Musgrove in this book for clarity, she was married three times and was also named Mary Matthews and Mary Bosomworth. She is the subject of several books.
3. *Colonial Records,* vol. 20, 88, 173, 373.
4. Coulter, *Journal of William Stephens,* vol. I, 149.
5. Coulter, *Journal of William Stephens,* vol. II, 129.

15. Unhappy Accidents

1. Coulter, *Journal of William Stephens,* vol. I, 97–98.
2. *Colonial Records,* vol. 20, 90.
3. *Colonial Records,* vol. 20, 32.
4. *Colonial Records,* vol. 20, 116. Maugre is an obsolete word meaning notwithstanding or in spite of.
5. *Colonial Records,* vol. 20, 33.
6. *Colonial Records,* vol. 20, 126.
7. *Colonial Records,* vol. 20, 164.
8. *Colonial Records,* vol. 20, 184.

16. Science And Beasts

1. *Journal of William Stephens,* vol. I, 201.
2. *Colonial Records,* vol. 4 supplement, 42.
3. Coulter, *Journal of William Stephens,* vol. II, 61.
4. *Colonial Records,* vol. 2, 167.
5. *Colonial Records,* vol. 4, 130.
6. *Colonial Records,* vol. 21, 158.

17. Dancing And Entertainments

1. *Colonial Records,* vol., 55.
2. *The Dancing Master; Or, Directions for Dancing Country Dances, with the Tunes to Each Dance, for the Treble-Violin* (London: Printed by J. Heptinstall, for H. Playford, 1698), https://www.loc.gov/item/11030463/.
3. *Colonial Records,* vol. 20, 230.
4. *Colonial Records,* vol. 4 supplement, 117–118.
5. Thomas Gamble, Jr., *A History of the City Government of Savannah, Ga, from 1790 to 1901 (Savannah: Under the Direction of the City Council, 1900)*, 53-54; "Curious Exhibition," *August Herald*, April 6, 1803, p. 3; "City Council Meeting Papers, City of Savannah, Georgi Records – Clerk of Council, Roll 5600CL–005 –02, 1790-1804.

18. Colonial Occupations

1. *Colonial Records,* vol. 4, 58–59.
2. *Colonial Records,* vol. 19, pt. I, 401.
3. Coulter and Saye, *A List of the Early Settlers,* 126; Anthony J. Turner, *The Time Museum,* vol. I (Rockford, Ill.: June 1984).
4. Cashin, *Setting Out,* 29; *Colonial Records,* vol. 4 supplement, 23–24.
5. *Colonial Records,* vol. 20, 92; Coulter and Saye, *A List of the Early Settlers,* 9.
6. Paul Bradshaw, "Silk Mill Secrets," BBC Criminal Histories, YouTube Video, 02:35, March 19, 2013, https://www.youtube.com/watch?v=HsFqKIk3T10

19. Troublesome Women

1. Coulter, *Journal of William Stephens,* vol. II, 83.
2. Coulter, *Journal of William Stephens,* vol. II, 163–245.
3. *Colonial Records,* vol. 6, 263–265.

20. Swamp Things

1. Alice Macgowan and Grace Macgowan Cook, *Return; a Story of the Sea Islands* (Boston: L.C. Page & Company, Inc., 1907), 206–207, https://www.loc.gov/item/05008709/.
2. Coulter, *Journal of William Stephens,* vol. II, 158.
3. *Colonial Records,* vol. 4, 128.
4. Gordon, *Colony of Georgia,* 40–41.
5. Gordon, 183.

6. E.R. Lanier, "Love, Law & Litigation in Colonial Georgia: The Trial and Tribulation of John Wesley in Savannah," *Journal of Southern Legal History* 13 (2005), 31–76.
7. Coulter, *Journal of William Stephens*, vol. II, 42, 208.
8. *Colonial Records*, vol. 21, 470.
9. Coulter, *Journal of William Stephens*, vol. I, 238–247.

21. Heartstrings

1. Coulter, *Journal of William Stephens*, vol. I, 90–91.
2. *Colonial Records*, vol. 4, 188–189.
3. *Colonial Records*, vol. 24, 313–314.
4. *Colonial Records*, vol. 20, 144–146.
5. "Letters from Georgia, vol. 14200," 66.
6. Coulter, *Journal of William Stephens*, vol. II, 136–137.

ABOUT THE AUTHOR

Grace Fleming was introduced to historical research by Savannah's beloved historian, Dr. Roger Warlick. Her first assignment was to write the biography of an anonymous person plucked from Savannah's archives. That one assignment began a long and enduring love of Savannah history.

Grace's publication and presentation topics include Savannah's African-American spies during the American Civil War, urban slavery, house histories of Savannah, and real pirates of Savannah.

Her fictional work includes *Celebrity Wedding in Flowery Branch* and *Paranormal Solved*.

Grace is currently working on a novel based on that very first research assignment. It is the story of an African woman who came to Savannah in 1790 and worked as a huckster to purchase her own freedom.

Made in the USA
Columbia, SC
04 October 2021

46655755R00096